DESIGNING YOUR SECOND LIFE

Techniques and inspiration for you to design your ideal parallel universe
within the online community, Second Life

New
Riders

REBECCA TAPLEY

Designing Your Second Life

Rebecca Tapley

With screenshots and additional content by Elana Angell

New Riders
1249 Eighth Street
Berkeley, CA 94710
510/524-2178
510/524-2221 (fax)

Find us on the Web at: www.newriders.com
To report errors, please send a note to errata@peachpit.com

New Riders is an imprint of Peachpit, a division of Pearson Education

Project Editor: Michael J. Nolan
Development Editor: Marta Justak
Production Editor: Tracey Croom
Proofreader: Liz Welch
Compositor: Kim Scott, Bumpy Design
Indexer: Rebecca Plunkett
Cover Designer: Mimi Heft
Interior Designer: Kim Scott, Bumpy Design

ISBN 13: 978-0-321-50301-5

ISBN 10: 0-321-50301-5

9 8 7 6 5 4 3 2 1

Printed and bound in the United States of America

This book is dedicated to Andrew, Elise, and Laura, who were born while I was writing—and to my sister, their mother, who carried them (nearly to term!) with tremendous grace under pressure. I love all of you, and I can't wait to see you.

Credits & Acknowledgements

This book, like Second Life itself, represents a tremendous collaborative effort.

First, many thanks to the people at Waterside Productions and New Riders/ Peachpit Press, especially Tracey Croom, Marta Justak, Michael Nolan, Rebecca Ross, Ming Russell, Sara Jane Todd, and everybody in the Production department. Thanks also to Elana Angell for contributing screenshots. This book would not have come into being without your time, patience, tenacity, advice, and expertise, and I'm very grateful.

I'm also grateful to all the Second Life residents who helped with my "scientific research." I did a Blanche DuBois, relying on the kindness of strangers to get opinions, product ratings, feedback on various tools and features, etc. without ever telling them why. As a result, the most important statistic I got to measure was the spontaneous generosity of the SL citizenry at large. I am very happy to report that 100 percent of respondents "tested" were willing to assist somebody they did not know. That says a lot about us as a community, and I'm prouder than ever to be part of SL as a result.

This is also my chance to acknowledge various friends and acquaintances who got me interested in gaming, and have continued to inspire me to think creatively, for the majority of my life: Erik Watson, John Verbrugge, David Kaiser; everybody from Hope College who played Cthulu in the basement of Voorhees Hall; Heather Gemmen; David Kennerly and all my friends from Nexus: Kingdom of the Winds and Dark Ages; and, most recently, the incomparable PJ Barry. Your imaginations kept mine percolating, and all those hours of fun and games (literally) helped lead me to this book. Thank you.

Thanks also to Amy Battisti-Ashe, Anna Callahan, Myfanwy Callahan, Matthew Glidden, Andrew Jaquith, Amy Lipman, and Sunny Schettler for persistently asking where the *$&?! I've been. Thanks for continuing to send me Evites, even though I had to bail on everything and write. See you at Felt! I'm buying!

Thanks especially to Erisavet Perway for introducing me to the online world of role-play (put down this book and go paint something *now*), and Vudu Suavage for being such an enthusiastic guide during my first visit to Second Life. Thank you also to the various artists and designers in Second Life who gave so much to the content of this book. You're not just supremely talented, but also incredible generous, and I'm thrilled to showcase your work here.

I had two fantastic "technical advisors" helping me get through the particularly sticky spots, namely Rod Campbell and Mina Pixie. Rod's command of Second Life miscellany is especially masterful, and his constant flow of URLs to newsy information helped keep my eye on the whole ball. Mina has an uncanny ability to hunt down, pounce on, and bring back the best of what Second Life stores have to offer. So I owe both of you especially heartfelt thanks. You're both in the details, and the details make this book a richer, more satisfying read.

Most importantly, all praise and high honors to my husband, Steve, for being the most gracious, forgiving, and patient Second Life widower in the multiverse. You constantly put up with the viral mess on the dining room table; you run to get pizza at the last minute; and you were instantly excited by the prospect of this book, even though it meant even more hours I'd have to spend glued to the laptop. So thank you, honey. The iPhone is on its way.

About the Author

Rebecca Tapley is an author, content management consultant, and jewelry designer in real life, and a virtual island developer in Second Life. Her career as a published writer covers business, graphic design, and Web site design software. Her consultancy client list includes Razorfish, Nexon USA, and Pearson Custom Publishing. Rebecca lives in metro Boston.

Register this Book

Register this book at www.peachpit.com/secondlife to gain access to the online appendix. Just log in and enter the ISBN, then a link to the appendix will be listed on your Account page.

contents

chapter 1

INTRODUCING YOUR SECOND LIFE

In the beginning (online)...there was text, and text was good. Email proved very useful. FTP sites made transferring large files quite easy. IRC chat gave birth to the almighty emoticon. ;-)

Next came the World Wide Web—text with pictures, and that was definitely better. The Web helped the Internet grow into one, powerful, *ginormous* encyclopedia of searchable information. Search engines such as Lycos, AltaVista, and Google made it possible for users and Web sites to find each other.

Not to mention the games. Elaborate, gorgeous games like Neverwinter Nights, Ultima Online, Everquest, and Worlds of Warcraft. Adventurers all over could play together—in real time!

Soon the corporate world opened its eyes. Shopping carts, live customer service, and PayPal made online commerce a reality. Successful, profitable companies such as eBay, Amazon, and Netflix came into existence and still exist solely because of the Internet.

Could it get any better, or more innovative?

Yes, it could, and it has: Second Life is here.

And Then There Was…Second Life

There is just nothing else like it. Right now, Second Life has been compared to New York City—a sprawling megalopolis/melting pot, constantly morphing and evolving, with new arrivals and developments and happenings occurring every day. The most fascinating part about SL is not necessarily what's already been done, either. What's most intriguing about SL is the endless creativity of its residents. Even the old-timers who've built exquisite houses, clothing, cars, and other such items keep trying new things—rebuilding and redesigning, pushing the envelope just a little more each and every day (see Figures 1.1–1.3 for just a taste).

FIGURE 1.1 The breathtaking world of Second Life…

FIGURE 1.2 …where no two places are alike…

FIGURE 1.3 …and very little seems impossible.

Getting Started: Just the Facts

Q: So what is Second Life?
A: Second Life is a 3D virtual online world with millions of residents, created and hosted by Linden Lab. It is populated by real people from all over the world interacting in real time, who are finding friends, having fun, designing art, and doing business. People—residents—are truly living another life in another world.

Q: How do I sign up?
A: Go to the Second Life Web site, sign up, and download the interface software. Your first account is free.

Q: For how long?
A: At this point, forever. There is no trial version, or limited access, or any other restriction on free accounts. You never have to pay for SL, in fact, unless you want to upgrade from a Basic (free) to a Premium (paid) account.

Q: Why should I upgrade to a Premium account?
A: There are two common, popular reasons why residents upgrade from a Basic to a Premium account: one, if they want to buy game money whenever they like, and two, if they want to buy land.

Q: Is the stuff available to residents with Basic accounts less interesting or not as cool?
A: Residents with Basic accounts can still go everywhere, build anything, buy anything, wear anything, and be anything they want. They can be paid or given Lindens from someone else, and they can rent land from another resident to live on. But the two main restrictions mentioned in the previous section here still apply.

Q: So, what's the storyline? How do you play?
A: Second Life has no storyline. There's no plot, no quests to go on, no monsters to slay, no levels to reach, no end or finale. In other words, there are no hoops to jump through to get to the good stuff. Second Life is *just* the good stuff.

Q: What kind of game has no storyline, plot, monsters, or anything else like that?
A: At a glance, Second Life does look like a game. However, Second Life does not embrace the rules or restrictions of a game, or force residents to perform tasks in order to get to the best that SL has to offer. SL is a completely open-ended world, and the only limitations you will encounter will be set by your time, curiosity, and imagination.

Q: Okay—I'm going to try it! What are the system requirements for my computer?
A: There are minimum system requirements and recommended system requirements spelled out on the Second Life Web site, for PCs running either Windows or Linux, and also for Macs. It's a very good idea to keep a close eye on this list, as Linden Lab constantly updates the SL interface to work with a greater variety of software and hardware components. (For example, at this writing, Second Life doesn't work with Windows Vista, but that will change very soon.)

With this purpose in mind, when you are crafting your Second Life, it is (and will be) very important for you to make thoughtful, informed design choices. Your avatar, your profile, your social connections, your residence, and even your career are all key elements to getting the most from your Second Life experience. Your avatar is definitely the key design project—the visual first impression you make in Second Life is a make or break moment (see Figures 1.4–1.6).

This idea might seem silly, especially if you are new to Second Life. However, if the current growth rate and popular interest in SL continues, more and more of your in-world activities may influence your real life and vice versa. Think about the World Wide Web. It began as a small network shared by just a handful of people with the same, specialized interests. If you weren't a particular type of scientist, or a particular type of U.S. government employee, the newborn Web was not important. You might think of Second Life much the same way, if you're not into computer games.

However, the Web soon began to blossom into the multilayered, multipurpose, essential resource it has become. For a time, lots of people hurried to play catch-up, and honestly, there are still a lot of Web sites out there that don't make the most of the medium. Second Life avatars have the same potential advantages and drawbacks. Your avatar can give others the impression that you're a savvy, experienced resident who can help someone else become the same thing. Or your avatar can do the opposite—convince someone else that you are a newcomer still trying to find your look, your niche, your purpose, and your balance.

FIGURE 1.4 You can be entirely human...

FIGURE 1.5 ...or half human...

FIGURE 1.6 ...or not human at all. It's your choice.

Personalizing Your Avatar: Just the Facts

Q: Linden Lab says my avatar is "infinitely customizable." Is that true?
A: It is! Beneath every single resident's appearance is a tweakable, human-shaped mesh. Almost every little area of this mesh can be adjusted with Second Life's Appearance tools, especially on the face. Then, over the top of this mesh in layers, you can add skin, hair, eyes, makeup, tattoos, and lots of other decorations. So it is very easy to make your avatar look just as you want it, via endless hours of customizing fun. Or you can go shopping and buy everything you want or need.

Q: Where do I get skin, hair, eyes, and all that?
A: Linden provides sets of all these essentials, along with the base avatar shape you choose when you sign up for your account. But if you want something different, you can find everything you need in SL's shops, designed and built by SL residents. If you'd rather not buy off-the-rack, many designers do custom work, too.

Q: What if I don't want to look human at all?
A: Not a problem—your avatar can look like anything real or unreal: a robot, a bluejay, a weird alien from outer space, a werewolf, a dinosaur, a dragon—or even a floating sparkly ball of light. You are only limited by your time, your imagination, and possibly your wallet.

There's more about this process, your choices, and some related recommendations on avatar design in Chapter 2, "Designing Your Avatar."

The purpose of this book, then, is to help you get ahead, and stay ahead, of the general learning curve. As Second Life continues to evolve into yet another online essential, there's a very good chance you will be adding the name of your SL avatar to your contact information, along with your email address and your AIM or MSN "handle." Chances are, also, that someday soon, you will use an SL avatar to attend a virtual business meeting or a lecture, to take a class, or to test or research real-world gadgets before going shopping at your local mall. This reality makes your first impression **in-world** into a crucial moment.

If these ideas are stressing you out, don't worry. Whether you are a newcomer to Second Life, or an established resident, you will find this book to be full of hints, strategies, and hidden gems that will help you sculpt your Second Life presence to perfection. This, in turn, will make you the true find, and the kind of resident others will want to approach with questions or just some friendly small talk. And these days, that stranger saying hello could be anybody: some sort of IT scout doing corporate reconnaissance, a Linden slumming undercover, or your next truly good friend. (There are many more details about designing the way your avatar looks, in both Chapter 2, "Designing Your Avatar," and in Chapter 3, "Designing Your Look.")

ʃLanguage

in-world *adj.* A common way residents, Lindens, and commentators describe or refer to something within Second Life, as opposed to "in-game," because SL is not, in fact, a game *and* many aspects of it are not quite game-like.

A Quick Overview of Second Life

As already mentioned in the Introduction, this book is not a how-to type of manual that approaches Second Life like software. This book is about optimizing your Second Life experience, above and beyond the tools, features, and technical controls, especially because how-to information is so widely and freely available. Linden Lab provides superior step-by-step help that's free of charge and completely available via the Knowledge Base and Community Forums—resources that are created and constantly refined by both Linden and residents alike.

However, if you want a nice summary of Second Life before you jump into the rest of this book, the remainder of this chapter is just for you. Here is a whirlwind tour of all the SL basics, from getting started to making friends, to building and finding and buying whatever your heart desires—and more.

Finding Your Way Around Second Life

The first sign of real interest and successful product design is a curious user. If you've become entranced by what you see and you want to learn more, you'll need to start searching and exploring. So now the goal is finding—finding all the tools and controls, finding out what you want your avatar to look like, finding other places and other people, and finding the fastest way from point A to point B.

The Second Life Interface

Once you create an account and get into Second Life (this process is covered in Chapter 2, "Designing Your Avatar"), you'll encounter the SL interface window. This should be your first exploration: figuring out where the controls are located and what they do.

There are two areas on the window where the tools and menus are located: along the top and the bottom (see Figure 1.7). The Chat text box is where you type what you want to say. The blue buttons along the very bottom work like shortcuts. Clicking them gives you quick access to some of the most frequently used features in SL, like the Build tools and the Snapshot camera for taking pictures. They are also the fastest way to get into everything in SL that's yours alone, such as the stuff in your Inventory and the names on your Friends list.

The drop-down menus (see Figure 1.8) along the top are the whole enchilada—all the creation, movement, search, view, and technical tools at your disposal.

FIGURE 1.7 The Second Life interface window with dialog boxes open.

FIGURE 1.8 A drop-down menu and all its related choices.

FIGURE 1.9 The almighty pie menu.

At the center, all the details about your present location are displayed, including icons that tell you if certain in-world features, such as flying, have been disabled. Near the upper-right corner, the in-world time is displayed, as is the balance of your in-world bank account. The tiny blue button in between is for buying Lindens (game money), and the vertical meters in the very corner are for measuring connection speed at a glance.

The third menu you'll use all the time is usually hidden from view until or unless you right- or Apple-click something. It's called the pie menu, because of its round shape and the way the tools on it appear (see Figure 1.9). These tools and features are all about interacting with objects in the Second Life world. If you click on your "self," you can use this menu to change clothes, tweak your appearance, and write/edit your profile. If you click on someone else, you can use the pie menu to view their profile, pay them money, or mute them if they are bothering you. If you click on an object, the pie menu brings up tools that allow you to return it to its owner, buy a copy if it's for sale, or peek at the names of the avatar that created it.

More information about individual tools and features is scattered throughout the book, as it relates to the different aspects of Second Life we're going to cover as we go. For a truly comprehensive tutorial on using the SL interface, visit the Forums and the Knowledge Base on the Second Life Web site at www. secondlife.com. There's also a considerable amount of helpful information in the Forums (also part of the SL Web site) and some nice, straightforward tutorials on Youtube—that's youtube.com, of course. These video tutorials are especially good if your question has to do with anything in SL that's in motion.

In Search of: Anything and Everything

After you've got your avatar's basic form squared away, you'll want to start dressing it up with better hair, clothes, eyes, skin, and maybe add some extras like tattoos or piercings. So now you know you can add all those unique touches to your appearance, but where do you find them?

Behold the power of Search (see Figure 1.10).

Second Life is so large, and it changes so often, that a Web-type search engine was the only answer for helping residents find what they wanted. So using the Search feature in-world is tremendously flexible, scalable, and responsive to whatever updates or other changes might happen to SL at large.

FIGURE 1.10 The Search tool: your SL search engine.

Let's start at one end of the Search process—the quest for results, because that's where an actual search begins—and work our way back to where and how such information is entered in.

You can use the Search feature by typing a keyword into the text box near the upper-left corner of the Search dialog box. Use a general category keyword like "shoes," or a more refined category term such as "women's shoes" (see Figure 1.11). You can type in an adjective description such as "goth" or "sk8rboi" to find items suitable for an entire head-to-toe style. Or, if you can be extremely specific, you can type in an avatar's name, a business or brand, or even the name of a region. (Search is covered more extensively in Chapter 4, "Designing Your Persona.")

When you get the list of results you want, just click on a choice in the left column and details will appear in the right. This is where searching turns into traveling—odds are, the place you want to go is far away from where you're standing. So how do you get from bare feet to haute couture? Take a second, closer look at Figure 1.11.

FIGURE 1.11 A Search results page: shoes, glorious shoes.

At the bottom-right corner of any Search results screen, there is a combination of names and numbers, which represents the location of (in this case) the shoe store you want to visit. There are also two blue buttons: Teleport and Show on Map. Teleport will instantly whisk you away to the place you found. Show on Map, on the other hand, allows you to preview your destination in detail with real-time information about what's going on in that region (see Figure 1.12).

The Map allows you to get lots of information, at a glance, about where you are and also where you want to visit next. As a natural next step to Search, the Map will display the shop or place advertised in Search results if you've clicked the Show on Map button. Your destination will appear in graphic format on the drawn map to the left, while more details about your destination and some travel options are accessible via tools on the right.

For immediate travel, the Map allows you to *teleport*, or jump immediately from your current location to the location brought up on the map by your Search efforts; click the blue Teleport button to make that happen. For future explorations, the Map also works as a way to save and keep teleportation "instructions" if you find a place you want to come back to in the future. These sets of instructions are called **landmarks** in-world and **SLURLs** in the real world.

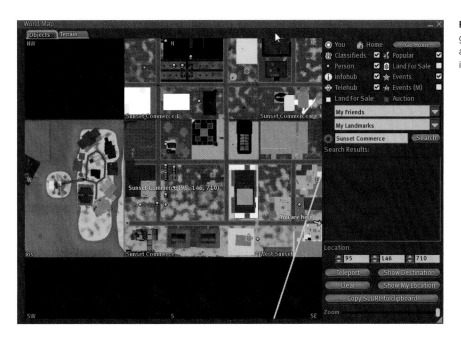

FIGURE 1.12 The Map: geographical, topographical, and other location information.

A landmark or SLURL is good for traveling across large stretches of the grid. But if you just want to explore your immediate surroundings, it's easiest to get around by walking, running, or flying. There are also carriages, sports cars, flying carpets, horses, and other "vehicles" to take you places, and they are lots of fun. But speedy travel is best accomplished under your own power.

Getting to Know You: SL Society and Culture

As you tool around Second Life, you're going to bump into strangers and strike up conversations. Some of these other people will be approachable and might even turn out to be friends. Others will be rude, crude, or otherwise off-putting, sometimes for no reason at all. If this sounds like real-life behavior in any crowded place, you're right on the money. SL is a society like any other, with expectations and assumptions about behavior, as well as do's and don'ts.

As far as Linden Lab is concerned, there are a handful of inviolable rules regarding the way residents should and should not treat each other. Breaking these rules can get you temporarily suspended or permanently booted from Second Life altogether, so pay attention. Linden calls these rules the community standards, or *The Big Six*, and here they are:

- **Intolerance**—Acting or speaking in such a way that "marginalizes, belittles, or defames" somebody based on his or her gender, sexual orientation, race, ethnicity, or religion.

- **Harassment**—It's not just sexual, especially not in a virtual world. Harassment is anything said or done that makes someone else feel alarmed, upset, intimidated, or uncomfortable. Don't do it—and don't press any issue if somebody says, "no."

- **Assault**—Pushing, shoving, shooting, attacking someone using something scripted, or otherwise making somebody uncomfortable in a safe area. If this is the type of activity you enjoy, go find an unsafe area and play with other likeminded residents who won't be bothered. (How do you tell the difference between safe and unsafe? If there's a heart-shaped icon at the top center of the Second Life window with a circle-slash through it, your avatar *could* be killed. There's more on this subject in Chapter 5, "Designing Your Social Life.")

- **Disclosure**—Privacy is quite possibly the most precious possession of every Second Life resident. So any action on your part that reveals an aspect of somebody's real-life identity that they have not shared publicly on their 1st Life Profile page (such as their location, marital status, gender, or even something like an IM username or email address) is called *Disclosure*. This is seriously, universally verboten, and even if Linden doesn't punish you, other residents will shun you for it.

- **Indecency**—Why are there PG- and Mature-rated areas within Second Life? So residents have a choice about exposing themselves to something potentially indecent. Pun intended. Keep it clean or go someplace M.

- **Disturbing the Peace**—If you do, say, build, or put something on the ground that makes a racket, you're disturbing the peace. Enough said, literally. Everybody has the right to quiet if they want it.

There's much more you should know about etiquette involved in Second Life society at large. We will cover general good advice on how to interact with others in Chapter 5.

Second Life Geography: Just the Facts

Q: How is land divided up in Second Life?

A: In order from smallest piece to largest area, Second Life land is divided by *parcel*, *region*, *estate*, *private island*, *microcontinent*, *mainland*, and *continent*. Here are the distinctions:

- A *parcel* of land is a discrete chunk of property measured in square meters, measuring anywhere between 512 sq/m (the smallest possible parcel) to 65,536 sq/m (the largest possible parcel). The word *parcel* is used in conversations about ownership, as only one person or group can own a parcel at one time. The rough real-world geographical equivalent of a parcel is a town or city.

- A *region* is Linden Lab's word for the largest possible parcel, i.e., whole and undivided at 65,536 sq/m. Every region has its own unique name, which gives it a distinct location in Search and on the various mapping tools within Second Life. In terms of real-life geography, a region is roughly equivalent to a state or a province.

- The term *estate* is used to describe all parcels of land owned by one resident or resident-created group. An estate also has its own discrete name, which may or may not be the same as one of the parcels made up by it. An estate can consist of just one parcel, or two or more on up to an infinite number of parcels; the largest estates in SL at this time contain over a thousand regions. So the rough equivalent to an estate in RL geography is a nation.

- A *private island* is a special-ordered type of whole region, requested and bought by a resident. The "island" part of the name refers to those regions' location on the grid at large—apart and separate from all of Linden's regions. However, at this writing, more and more residents are investing in multiple private islands that sit side by side.

- A *microcontinent* is, at this writing, a relatively new term used to describe some chains or clusters of private islands. Microcontinents are not just located together on the grid. They are specifically developed and designed to look like one seamlessly continuous piece of land. Most microcontinents are platforms for business ventures, such as residential real estate, or for cooperative socializing purposes, such as role-playing. Pundits and analysts speculate the number of microcontinents will continue to rise.

- *Mainland* is the in-world opposite to private islands. It describes regions that Linden created and continue to create as Second Life expands. Mainland property is for sale or for rent just like private island property, but to a lesser extent because the Lindens maintain ongoing ownership. "Mainland" is often used as a comparative adjective, too, when describing the evolution of SL land in general, as mainland is the oldest land in the SL world.

- Last but not least, a *continent* is the largest land mass in Second Life. Continents are massive Linden-created megaclusters of regions, created and designed to look as true-to-life as possible. Continents are excellent examples of everything possible in land development and terraforming, with wide, contiguous transition in sea level from ocean shores to mountaintops; climate variety from desert to snowscape; and all sorts of natural wonders such as gorges and waterfalls.

Take This Job and Love It: Your SL Career

In most "games" or virtual worlds, you have no hope of acquiring or spending game money unless the game/world designers allow you to do so—and this process is often boring, frustrating, slow, or otherwise no fun whatsoever. Second Life is three hundred and sixty degrees different. Not only do you get Lindens (game money) from Linden Lab every month just for being a resident. You can either purchase game money outright using the L$ button in the upper-right

The Second Life Economy: Just The Facts

Q: Let me get this straight: you can buy game money anytime you want?

A: Yes. You don't have to reach a certain goal or complete a certain task, not even the full tutorial on Help Island.

Q: What if I have a free account?

A: You do need to have a Premium account, for example, some sort of payment information on file, to be able to purchase game currency commonly known as *Lindens* (and officially known as *Linden dollars*).

Q: What if I'm new to Second Life?

A: There is a sliding scale for currency purchase limits, depending on how long you've been a resident—one day or less, 2 to 13 days, 14 to 27 days, and longer. The limits on how many Lindens you can sell/exchange for real-life currency are determined by the same limitations. However, the amounts of money you can buy and sell have recently changed and will change again. As Linden Lab raises its monthly charges and other expenses (such as the price of buying private islands), these upper limits have to increase as well in order to allow residents to spend Lindens freely.

Q: How do I buy Lindens?

A: To buy Lindens, click the round blue button labeled 'L$' in the upper-right corner of the Second Life Interface window. The Buy Currency dialog box will pop open, where you can see the current exchange rate and also type in how many Lindens you want to buy. SL automatically calculates how much real-life money you'll be charged before you click Purchase, too, so you know exactly what you're spending and receiving. The cost of your currency purchase will appear on the statement for whatever credit card, bank account, or PayPal account you used to open your Premium account.

Q: How do I sell Lindens?

A: Go to the Second Life Web site, sign in, and click the oval blue button about halfway down the left side labeled "Buy and Sell Linden Dollars." This process places a Sell Currency order on the LindeX, or Linden currency exchange, and deposits the real-life currency (U.S. dollars, euros, etc.) into your Second Life account.

corner of the SL interface window. Or you can also earn Lindens quickly and easily by just sitting in a chair, dancing on a disco pad, or filling out a survey.

If you have just a touch more time, interest, and motivation, you can get an actual job in Second Life. Some even pay you in real-life currency, depending on the hours you put in, the kind of work you do, and who your employer is. Some jobs are admittedly racy by some people's standards—there's sex and gambling throughout the Mature areas of Second Life, just like there are similarly themed Web sites out on the Web at large. But there are also all sorts of other occupations—from DJing to modeling on the catwalk to planning or performing weddings—that are fun and interesting and even lucrative if you get really good.

There's much more information about earning, buying, selling, and otherwise using Lindens as your salary in Chapter 6, "Designing Your Home." (Figure 1.13 displays the Classifieds listings where you'll find a job.)

FIGURE 1.13 The Classifieds listings: how to finance your Second Life.

Home Sweet Home: Finding a Place to Live

If you get a job in Second Life, why not also find yourself a place to live? Second Life real estate is just like its real-life counterpart in some ways. You can rent, you can buy, you can pay someone to build your dream house, or you can buy a ready-made house you just plunk down and move into (see Figure 1.14).

Ultimately, the question is how much? How much space, how much to spend, how much stuff to buy, how much time to invest? It all depends on your mood, your preferences, and your passion. There are residents living in one-room shacks, replicas of real-world royal palaces, space stations, genie bottles, tree houses, and even carved-out coral reefs. So if anything is possible, the only question you need to contemplate is how far you want to go.

Almost everybody starts small, with just a tiny parcel or studio-type apartment. In the beginning, it's more fun to browse, window-shop, and figure out what kind of styles, colors, and forms appeal to you. This can take a long time, and a lot of wandering. Every type of furniture, carpet, tapestry, knick-knack and decorative item that's ever been created in the real world—and quite a few

FIGURE 1.14 Live in your dream home (or apartment, or condo, or...)

that don't exist outside SL— is here for the buying. The shops of Second Life are a tempting buffet of everything you've ever wanted for any part of your living space—even the garage, the backyard, the heliport, or the dungeon.

There's more information about renting and buying Second Life property towards the end of the book, along with introductory material on how to build your own residence. Look at Chapter 6, "Designing Your Home," Chapter 7, "Designing Your Homestead," and Chapter 8, "Designing Your Empire."

Second Life Real Estate: Just the Facts

Q: How do I find a place to live in Second Life?
A: Real estate in Second Life isn't terribly different from real estate in real life. First, decide if you want to rent or buy and take it from there.

Q: I want to rent a place to live. How does that work?
A: Use Search to look around at all the places that match your criteria. Then set up the payment process—some landlords ask you to pay with PayPal, some will take payment directly, and others use a scripted object that accepts Lindens. Typically, you'll have to pay both rent on the living space and a *tier fee*, or monthly maintenance charge that's scaled by land size. (Think of it like owning a condominium in real life; you'd pay the mortgage to the bank and a fee to the condo association, too.)

Q: Okay, I'd rather buy a place to live instead. How does that work?
A: Again, you have several options. You can buy mainland property, or part of a private island, or pay Linden Lab to create an entire private island to your specifications. However, you should add in the cost of upgrading your account from Basic to Premium if your Second Life account is currently free.

Q: What should I know about buying mainland property?
A: You'll pay a lump sum amount to the seller for the property, and you'll pay that tier fee to Linden Lab in addition to the monthly charge for your Premium account.

Q: What should I know about buying private island property?
A: Private island property is owned by a resident rather than Linden Lab, although the two-fee structure is also most common—a lump sum outright plus the monthly tier. However, if you buy private island land, your monthly payment to Linden Lab will not go up.

Q: What should I know about buying an entire private island?
A: It's expensive—the most expensive type of property you can purchase in Second Life when all the costs are totaled up. The best part is, the entire 65,536 sq/m will be yours, completely private if you want, like your own little sanctuary or personal kingdom. But on the other hand, the tier fee is several hundred dollars U.S. in addition to the Premium account fee. So a private island is a pricey indulgence, unless you have a plan to use it for commercial space somehow.

From Sunglasses to Skyscrapers: Second Life's Amazing Build Tools

Most Second Life residents also try their hand, at some point, at building something. The possibilities are just too intriguing. The SL Build tools make it feasible to build something as small as a nose ring, as large as the Eiffel Tower, or anything imaginable in between (see Figure 1.15).

The best way to learn the Build tools is by doing, and fortunately Second Life encourages this kind of hands-on experimentation. There are numerous places to go and take or read building tutorials. There are many areas called *sandboxes*, where you can tweak and tinker as much as you want without paying a cent.

There are also many, many talented builders who teach classes in-world and manage the Build-related forums. So go ahead and give the Build tools a trial run. At the very least, it will give you something to talk about with other residents and help you break the conversational ice.

FIGURE 1.15 The wonderful, flexible, powerful Build tools.

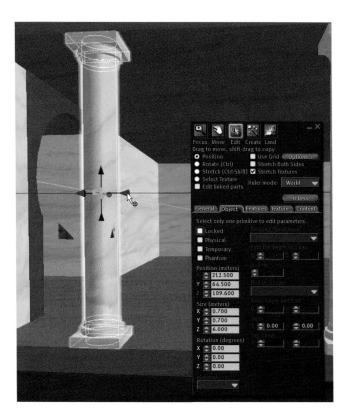

Building in Second Life: Just the Facts

Q: Who can build in Second Life?
A: Everybody! Building in Second Life is not limited to a select handful of high-level, administrative, or GM-type residents. It's a universal, equal-opportunity activity.

Q: How does building work?
A: To put it very simply, building in Second Life is a lot like playing with blocks. Linden Lab provides a set of basic shapes called primitives or *prims*, which can be changed in size with the editing tools and changed in appearance by adding colors or textures. Then you take your customized prims, arrange them in whatever collective form you want them to take, and link them together to lock them in place. That's building in a nutshell. All it takes is practice (lots and lots of it, but still, just practice).

Q: Where do you find or buy prims?
A: No finding or buying required: anybody can create prims using the Build tools. There's no per-prim cost. There's no limit on how many prims a resident can make. There's no limit to how many prims you can keep in your Inventory. However, if you want to keep the things you build with prims, it's a different story.

Q: How do I keep things I've built?
A: There are two ways to keep what you create. You can put the finished linked object into your Inventory and give it a distinct name; use the General tab page in the Edit dialog box. Or you can build the object in question on land you are renting or owning. The *number* of prims you can permanently set down and keep on a piece of land does vary, though. The SL grid is programmed to host or support a limited number of prims per square meter, and there's no way around it.

Remember, there's plenty of advice on building and all the associated design tasks that go along with it, depending on how much land you have, such as landscaping and terraforming, in Chapters 6, 7, and 8.

Thus endeth the introduction to *Designing Your Second Life*. The very next chapter will help you design a better-looking avatar, or in-game version of yourself, whether you are starting from scratch or trying to refine what you already have.

ADDITIONAL CREDITS

You can find all the brand, style, color, and designer information on items shown in the figures in the online appendix you get when registering your book at at www.peachpit.com/secondlife. See page v for details.

chapter 2

DESIGNING YOUR AVATAR

2

When you see an avatar in Second Life, you're viewing the persona that particular resident of SL wants to project—a summary of his interests, personalities, goals, aspirations—the purpose, ultimately, of a cyberlife.

This premise might be hard to grasp, as people often think "game" when looking at cartoon-like, human-shaped figures. Even if you customized that figure and gave it your unique stamp, your brain says that figure can't possibly be "me."

Residents of Second Life who think this way are pretty easy to spot. In some fashion, they have an attitude indicating they aren't interested in SL as a cooperative experience. Detail makes all the difference in the way someone designs an avatar, and creating detail takes intention, time, and planning.

In this chapter, you'll learn about the foundation components of your avatar—shapes, skins, eyes, hair, additional attachments, and finishing touches. In the process, you'll develop a better understanding of how and why detail is created, while viewing specific samples of avatar design.

Some Assembly Required: Constructing Your Avatar

When you look at an avatar, you are also looking at examples of the two primary ways to create three-dimensional detail in Second Life. One way is with texture, or surface pattern, alone. The other is with the judicious use and manipulation of prims. In fact, the way that residents choose to create, shape, and accessorize their avatars says a lot about what they understand about SL design in general.

A Second Life **avatar** is assembled in layers, with a mesh at the very foundation. In Second Life parlance, the mesh in your avatar is called its *shape*, a collection of prims put together to resemble the human body. Every other part of your avatar, from skin to hair to eyes, is added to the shape in turn. The collective effect of all these components is what gives your avatar its unique and finished look. So let's look at each part of your avatar, starting at the bottom-most layer—the shape—and working our way up.

Choosing Your Name

Choosing your name might seem like a momentary decision, but you should give it a little thought.

Technically speaking, there are only a few restrictions:

- First names may be 2 to 31 characters long.
- First names may include letters and numbers, but not symbols or spaces.
- First names cannot be R-rated; you'll get an error message saying the name is invalid and be prompted to try something else.
- Last names are preselected; you only get to choose from the list Linden provides (unless you want to pay big bucks for a vanity name).

In reality, there are other considerations worth thinking about. The name of your avatar can never, ever be changed—and an avatar you create will never be deleted. So a poor choice on your part will become a permanent indignity. What makes a poor choice? A word containing numbers (considered very newbie), a word that is a brand name or contains one (a copyright no-no), or a word that's hard to spell or difficult to remember (why make it tough for others to find you?).

Basic Anatomy: Your Avatar's Shape

Altering your avatar's shape affects the appearance of everything else layered on top of it. This, in turn, will fool the eye into perceiving body parts a little bit differently. It may also affect your choices of hair, clothing, and other items that are worn on different parts of your avatar's body. In fact, some of the body parts pictured in these figures are actually created and worn as clothing. Clothing is layered over various parts of your avatar to create different outfits and effects, the same way that body parts and skin are layered over the shape. (For more details on how clothing works in this design process, turn to Chapter 3, "Designing Your Look.")

If it sounds like this learning curve is too daunting, don't worry. In general, Second Life's Appearance tools do prevent you from making a mess of things. First, each Appearance tool is controlled by a slider bar. So you will always be able to see where you are headed if you keep nudging the slider bar to either the left or the right (see Figure 2.1).

By changing the position of a slider bar, you are altering the dimensions of a group of prims, not each tiny prim individually. If you change the height of your avatar, for example, that slider setting will proportion your entire shape accordingly. The head, arms, and torso areas of the mesh will all stretch and

ʃLanguage

prim *n.* Short for "primitive." It refers to the basic building blocks that are provided in various logical shapes, such as cubes, cones, and spheres—and supported by the Second Life grid. Prims make up everything in-world from the smallest piece of jewelry to the most enormous, elaborate castle. They are also the true currency and source of greed within SL culture, because the number of prims at your disposal will either free or limit your imagination.

FIGURE 2.1 The Appearance menu tools.

resize in relation to your avatar's longer legs. You won't have to readjust each part of your avatar's body individually.

Second, there's always the Revert button at the bottom of the Appearance dialog box, too, if you really go too far with your changes. For that matter, there's also the Randomize button if you want to play with all the slider settings at once, just to see what happens. The point is that you really cannot make an irredeemable mess of your avatar's shape. So go ahead and play with all the individual settings, and see what each of them creates, both alone and in relation to the other areas on the shape around the one you are changing.

If you get frustrated trying to sculpt your shape and you can't quite figure out why, consider this fact of virtual design. The real human body has tendons, ligaments, cartilage, and muscles that provide "padding" between the skeleton and the skin. However, there's nothing padding-like between the mesh and your avatar's skin, even though such an additional layer would make an avatar look much more true-to-life.

A Second Life avatar lacks these extras for technical reasons: it's easier for the SL servers to render and animate a more simply constructed, "unpadded" figure. Unfortunately for SL residents (and fortunately for certain designers), this measurement restriction makes creating your own shape one of the most difficult design tasks in-world. In fact, some areas of your avatar's body will never look quite right, no matter how hard you work on or look for the perfect base shape. The shoulder sockets, elbows, fingers, knees, and toes will never be more than a rough approximation of the real thing, until or unless Linden makes alterations to the mesh.

➜ General Design Tip: The Face

If you have your heart set on looking different from everyone else in Second Life, the easiest way to accomplish this goal is to start with the shape of your avatar's face. The vast majority of female avatars in SL have oval-shaped faces, and the vast majority of male avatars in SL have squared or rectangular faces. So you can quickly distinguish yourself from the pack by making slight, but significant, changes to the forehead, cheekbones, and jawline of your avatar's face.

Choosing a Starter Shape

After you choose a first and last name for yourself (and put in all the real-life information Linden Lab requires for, you know, payment), then it's time to choose your basic shape. Unlike your name, you can change the base shape of your avatar very easily. You even have all 12 base shapes in the Library folder in your Inventory, male and female, regardless of what shape you choose when you create your account (see Figures 2.2–2.5).

Most residents choose the human-looking base shapes to start their selection process—for example, the Next Door, City Chic, or Nightclub options. For one thing, most of Second Life is designed and scaled to accommodate human-looking avatars. This means it can really help to have a human base shape to work with as a newcomer, so you can become familiar with the proportion and scale of the SL environment.

FIGURE 2.2 (from left to right) City Chic—Male, Boy Next Door, and Harajuku—Male basic avatar shapes, skins, and body parts.

FIGURE 2.3 (from left to right) The Cybergoth—Male, Furry—Male, and Nightclub—Male basic avatar shapes, skins, and body parts.

FIGURE 2.4 (from left to right) The Nightclub—Female, Girl Next Door, and City Chic—Female basic avatar shapes, skins, and body parts.

FIGURE 2.5 (from left to right) The Cybergoth—Female, Furry—Female, and Harajuku—Female basic avatar shapes, skins, and body parts.

If this is your first avatar, you should also consider the learning curve. How much time do you have to spend in Second Life? Even if you're a quick study, it will take you a while to get the hang of Second Life's Search, Appearance, and other features. That's time you will probably have to spend in long stretches doing tweaking, making mistakes, and starting over. Are you planning on trying to find an out-of-the-way corner first, where you can hide out until your transformation is complete? (Not likely.)

The other way to go, of course, is to buy everything from your shape on up. The challenge with this plan is time. Even if you think shopping is fun and can't wait to get started, it's going to take a while to find what you want because SL is so vast. There are also a mind-boggling array of shapes, skins, eyes, and hair for sale in Second Life—to say nothing of clothes and accessories. Fortunately SL has a powerful, yet easy-to-use Search feature. Search is covered in detail in Chapter 4, "Designing Your Persona."

At first, you also won't know the difference between items that are unique and well designed, and items that are boring and poorly designed. You have to be patient and look around for a while. So the potential cool factor of choosing a nonhuman base shape is somewhat lessened by all these facts. You're going to have plenty to do, and plenty you'll want to do, without having to "fix" your avatar as soon as possible.

We already covered the limitations of the mesh at the beginning of this chapter, but there is a second reason why your avatar won't look perfectly realistic—light. The ambient light within the Second Life environment catches every bump, curve, and dent in your avatar's shape, for better and for worse. A truly good shape can camouflage some of these hard angles, or even use ambient light to its advantage. So let's examine and consider the details that make some shapes superior to others.

Choosing a Female Shape

Take a look at these examples of real women in Figures 2.6–2.8.

In Second Life, female human avatar shapes are actually easier to make than male human shapes. This is because the basic anatomy of a woman's body has an hourglass form, which is easily constructed with elongated oval prims. It doesn't matter if you want your avatar to be supermodel-thin, sporty-buff, or generously curved. The female avatar form is flattered by Second Life's ambient light. See Figures 2.9–2.11, which show three good general examples.

There's an old adage that says, just because you can, doesn't mean you should, and frankly, this sentiment applies to choosing a female human shape. You can design or buy a female shape with breasts that defies gravity, physiological common sense, and even some definitions of good taste. (You will certainly

©iStockphoto.com/Branislav Ostojic

FIGURE 2.6 The female human body: long lines...

©iStockphoto.com/Oleksandr Gumerov

FIGURE 2.7 ...gentle curves...

©iStockphoto.com/Izabela Habur

FIGURE 2.8 ...elongated ovals.

FIGURE 2.9
Copyright Mallory Cowen (eyes), Fia Hartunian (shape), Santana Lumiere (skin), Jeremy Majestic (swimsuit), and Cay Trudeau (hair).

FIGURE 2.10
Copyright Laydi Bailly (hair), Christine Debs (shape), Santana Lumiere (eyes), Alaska Metropolis (swimsuit), Portia Sin (manicure), and Distar Wakawaka (skin)

FIGURE 2.11
Copyright Mallory Cowen (eyes), Zyrra Falcone (hair), Don Proost (shape), Andromeda Raine (swimsuit), and Ryntha Suavage (skin).

look good in your club clothes if you do.) But you should also consider buying or designing another shape you can wear every day, something less eye- and seam-popping. You never know when you might want or need to project a different kind of image, and a little forethought up-front means you won't be scrambling to find a normal look later on.

So, what is "normal" for a female human avatar shape in Second Life? Think about the classic hourglass or the flowing curvature of a violin. From the front, the narrowest part of your avatar's trunk should be the waist, but not drastically. Generally speaking, you want to pay more attention to the design of your avatar's upper half anyway, because that's where other residents will look at her. Every time your avatar speaks aloud in Second Life, she will start making typing motions—lifting her hands up to keyboard height, palms down, and wiggling her fingers. This distinct and somewhat peculiar movement draws a lot of attention to the upper third of your avatar's body.

It also, eventually, prompts the brain to make certain comparisons between similarly shaped features. If your avatar's eyes and mouth are noticeably identical in diameter, your avatar's face will look less convincingly realistic. For similar reasons, if your female avatar has breasts that are too rounded and too large, your female avatar's head will actually look too small.

Another classic mistake is positioning the breasts too high on the rib cage. You want to draw a vertical line between your avatar's navel and the hollow at the base of her throat, and divide that space horizontally into thirds. Your avatar's nipples should be aligned with the boundary between the first and second thirds, no lower (think post-partum droop) and no higher (think discount plastic surgery).

Choosing a Male Shape

Now, for contrast, let's look at these examples of the male human body in Figures 2.12–2.14.

Replicating the male human body as an avatar, as opposed to replicating the female human body, is a trickier proposition. Notice that a man's muscles are more individually distinct, creating hills and valleys. Depending on which area of the male body you consider, each muscle is either more angled and flat, or more domed, than a woman's. There's far less gradual gradation to the lines of a man's body, which means a male avatar's musculature can easily look lumpy.

Figures 2.15–2.17 reveal the differences in how Second Life's ambient light treats the male-shaped avatar.

So what makes a good male shape? Proportion. If you want to bulk up and look like an extra from *Conan the Barbarian*, don't just add muscle to your avatar's upper arms, thighs, and chest. Increase the size of your avatar's hands and feet, thicken the neck and the waist, and pad the calf and triceps muscles for balance.

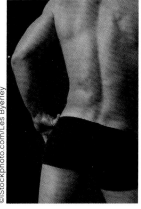

FIGURE 2.12 The male human body: flat surfaces...

FIGURE 2.13 ...sharper angles...

FIGURE 2.14 ...a bumpy silhouette.

FIGURE 2.15
Copyright Devlin Davis (shape), Unsub Hoi (eyes), Tami McCoy (hair), Aimee Weber (shorts), and Canimal Zephyr (skin).

FIGURE 2.16
Copyright June Dion (hair), Unsub Hoi (eyes), Lion Valentino (trunks), and Vindi Vindaloo (skin).

FIGURE 2.17
Copyright Zen Deledda (trunks), Fia Hartunian (eyes), and Lost Thereian (hair, shape, and skin).

You should also play to the stereotype of the D&D Warrior and choose a long hairstyle. Remember, most residents who encounter your avatar will be summing it up at a glance, for better or for worse. So, just go with the fact that we've all been preprogrammed by movies, console games, and paperback romance covers. Get your guy some long hair and evoke the mystique of "The Gorgeous Hunk."

If you want your male human avatar to look more middle-of-the-road and normal, the trick again is proportion but to a less extreme degree. Imagine that your avatar is still ripped, but try to picture him relaxing in a recliner watching ESPN. In other words, imagine all those big muscles are not bulging. Imagine them smoother and lying closer to the bone—still evident, but not permanently flexed. If you can focus on this mind-image when choosing a shape, your male avatar will end up looking less obviously fake or phony.

Basic Anatomy: Your Avatar's Skin

There are many skins for sale in Second Life that look identical to the real thing, complete with a blush in the cheeks, day-old stubble and scars, and even a sprinkling of freckles. But the basic purpose of your avatar's skin is not necessarily to look true to real life. The basic purpose of your avatar's skin is to make up for the limitations of the shape underneath it.

We already touched briefly on the effects of Second Life's ambient light. From the example bodies shown here, you saw how many shape designers do their best to compensate for the lack of padding by carefully adjusting the mesh. These adjustments can smooth out the dents and dips between individual prims on the mesh. But it is still very difficult to create realistic-looking fine detail without shading, drawn or painted in just the right places, on the skin.

The best-looking female human skins have some shadowing between the breasts, around the navel, and around the natural curves of the buttocks. The operative word here, however, is *some*. A skin that attempts to create too much definition, of the breasts and buttocks, in particular, will not always resize properly if you choose to make your avatar either very slender or very muscular.

The hardest skin to find in Second Life, hands-down, is a simple, well-designed, human male skin. From these examples, you can see that a lot of design attention is often paid to the "six-pack" of abdominal muscles between the ribcage and navel, and to the buttocks. Sometimes, additional contouring is provided to the upper chest and arms, as well as the shoulderblades. But additional realistic details, such as body hair on the arms or legs, are not easy to find.

General Design Advice: Naughty Bits

If the Barbie or Ken appearance of your naked avatar alarms you, there's no need to scour your Inventory or contact Help. Shapes and skins in Second Life do *not* come with naughty bits. You have to buy them separately and put them on, just like your hair, eyes, and other anatomical parts.

If you want nipples for your avatar, male or female, you have to buy or make a skin that includes them. Many skins are available that come with nipples (and navels, for that matter) painted or drawn on in just the right places. There are also three-dimensional nipples for both genders, although most of them are sold with piercings to make the studs or hoops fit properly.

Female genitalia are most often, also, painted or drawn on the skin unless piercings are involved. Male genitalia, on the other hand, are always built and sold as three-dimensional **attachments** that appear and stay, again, in just the right place.

A word to the wise here: if you purchase 3D naughty bits, you will always have to remember to take them off. Otherwise, they will be visible over your clothes. Men should be especially aware of this particular faux pas, as you could easily be mistaken as a troublemaker running around with his fly open, bent on indecent exposure.

Everybody should be aware that the most popular brands of naughty bits are scripted to be interactive. These nipples, genitalia, and other sensual attachments are clickable by and responsive to other people. So if someone else rests his or her cursor on some part of your avatar's body where naughty bits are located, your parts will "describe" quite explicit reactions out loud in open chat. Also very embarrassing.

Fortunately, you can turn yourself off (pun intended here), if you attach your naughty bits to your avatar and click on them yourself. This will cause a menu to appear in the upper-right corner of your screen, with several owner options including a "disable" or "ignore" type setting. For more information on how to manage your naughty bits, read the Help notecards included in the vended box you received during purchase.

ſLanguage

attachment *n.* An object or group of objects that hangs or sits on your avatar. The most popular attachments simulate some 3D part of the anatomy (like naughty bits or hair), clothing, jewelry, or something carried (like a sword, purse, or bouquet of flowers). There are 30 places on your avatar where attachments can be placed. But it's very common to have to choose between wearing two attachments, such as bracelets and shirt cuffs, if they are designed to attach in the same location.

Basic Anatomy: Hair and Eyes

In one way, Second Life is just like real life: most residents look at an avatar's face first. So it pays to give serious thought to how you want to "top off" the look of your shape and skin. Your eyes and hair might be the first thing someone else notices about your avatar, for better or for worse.

Choosing Hair

Second Life hair is nothing but fun. It takes absolutely no maintenance. It comes in every conceivable color. Some extremely talented Second Life designers have spent hours creating every possibly style, so you have hundreds of options to choose from.

Let's take a look at these examples in Figures 2.18 and 2.19 to get an idea of what's out there.

The majority of resident-designed hairstyles are made up of two or more individual pieces, not just one. The foundation, which goes on first, is the "bald cap," which covers your avatar's entire scalp and often the forehead as well. This piece is particularly important if you are keeping your Linden-created skin, which more than likely has hair painted onto the head.

The bald cap also repositions the eyebrows to a more natural or sculpted position on the face, or changes the eyebrow color to match the hair it accompanies. In fact, if you find you prefer one designer's bald cap, feel free to mix and match

FIGURE 2.18
Copyright Mallory Cowen (eyes), Jenna Fairplay (shape), Sibele Ingmann (hair) and Santana Lumiere (skin) and Polyester Partridge (earrings).

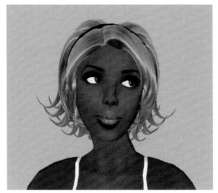

FIGURE 2.19
Copyright Mallory Cowen (skin), Namssor Daguerre (eyes), Radiant Jewel (hair), and Gala Phoenix (shape).

General Design Advice: Buying Hair

- Hairstyles often come in multiple pieces, so always check your purchase and be sure you have everything you need. This is especially important if you buy a "pack" of identical hairstyles in different colors.
- Almost every hair salon in SL selling resident-designed hairstyles offers demos, available either for free or for L$1. It is highly advisable to take your time and try on the demos of everything you like before you buy.
- Use the Camera Controls or a posing stand to look at yourself wearing a demo from every angle. It's easy to forget that the most important angle of a hairstyle is the front—which is what everyone else will usually see first—rather than the back, which is what you look at all the time.
- If you like to wear lots of decorative items on your head, don't buy a hairstyle that comes in multiple pieces. A multipart hairstyle just increases the likelihood that something will compete for attachment with your jewelry, piercings, eyelashes, tattoos, glasses, or headgear.

it with every hairstyle you buy. The bald cap object itself will work with any hairstyle object, with no technical issues involved.

The most popular hair designers in Second Life agree that long hairstyles for women sell the best. This is especially true since Linden made "flexi" or flexible prims available. Long hair designed with flexi prims can flow and bend around the upper body in a much more realistic fashion. Shorter hairstyles are still, most commonly, made from nonflexi prims, which are easier to work with and look natural when used for such design.

However, extremely short hairstyles are very hard to re-create realistically and therefore very hard to find (see Figure 2.20). Buzz cuts and military-style short hair for men pose a particular challenge to Second Life designers. Such styles tend to look too flat if they are painted on the scalp, and they require too many individual pieces to be feasible if designed by attaching prims (see Figure 2.21).

FIGURE 2.20
Copyright Dorian Doigts (eyes), Launa Fauna (skin), Fia Hartunian (shape), Six Kennedy (hair), and Wednesday Rejected (piercings).

Choosing Eyes

While your avatar's hair can be made up from dozens or even hundreds of individual prims, its eyes are more or less flat, single pieces. Many eye designers invest a lot of time in making their textures look as real as possible. They size and scale the pupils, they draw glass-like reflections on the surface of the eyeball, and they even add tiny veins in the whites. These types of eyes are a

FIGURE 2.21
Copyright Fonix Frua (skin) and Charlotte Hausdorf (eyes).

good choice if you are going for a subdued, real-life kind of avatar, or for your everyday look.

Other designers concentrate on producing striking, saturated colors on the verge of seeming unrealistic. On the "shelf," these eyes might look too bright or intense to seem workable. But when you combine them with glamorous makeup, vividly colored hair, or supermodel fashion, such eyes will complete your look rather than overwhelm it.

Then there are the fantasy eyes—the ones that go well beyond anything considered normal, from the vampiric and animal to the gothic and anime-inspired. If you're going to go nonhuman altogether, you will need just the right eyes as the icing on the cake. The best way to choose wisely is to observe what other furries, nekos, zombies, cyborgs, lycans (or whatever your species of choice)

General Design Advice: Finishing Touches

You can also add nail polish, facial hair, and makeup to your avatar very easily, as "tattoos" applied to specific parts of the skin, or as prims attached to specific parts of the body. The most important consideration for all these finishing touches is contrast. Consider, for example, matching facial hair to the darkest strands in your hair, especially if you have fair skin.

Makeup should *not* match your eye color; opposing shades, such as browns and purples paired with green or blue eyes, will make your eye color "pop" appropriately, especially if your lipstick of choice is dark or very glossy.

Nail polish is available for your fingers and your toes, in everything from French tips to chrome blue to blackest black. The palest shades of polish will just plain disappear most of the time, because of the way ambient light plays off your avatar's fingers. So avoid pastels and beige, and go for all those bright, strong, funky colors.

An effective, yet subtle trick, is to match your fingernail color to your eyes as closely as possible. Alternatively, wear all-black tribal tattoos on your arms if your avatar has black hair, or henna designs on your hands if your avatar has warm red in her hair. Remember your hands will be hovering at chest level whenever you "talk," because of the keyboard typing animation. So coordinating colors will draw others' eyes down to your avatar's hands, and then to your whole look.

FIGURE 2.22

FIGURE 2.23

are wearing. Then ask that resident and explain that you admire their avatar's ensemble. Most often, the person will respond in a friendly way and tell you where to go shopping.

Alternative Anatomy: Going Semi-Human

If just plain human feels, well, just too plain, there are many, many ways to go semi-human—to transform your avatar into something else with two arms and two legs that doesn't look normal. Figures 2.22–2.24 are just a handful of all the choices out there at your disposal.

FIGURE 2.24

All these example semi-human avatars are, in fact, recognizably human base shapes. They are still, more or less, human in form and human in size. The additional parts that make these avatars into something unusual are attachments. "Regular" humans might only require hair and naughty bits to complete that look. "Semi-humans," like these avatars, can require dozens of them.

If or when you buy a complicated avatar like any of these semi-human examples, chances are good you'll receive a single, vended box in exchange for your money. Don't worry; you've gotten exactly what you need. A single container-like object is a common way for Second Life designers to distribute items made up of several pieces.

To open a container, drag it from your Inventory onto the ground (in an area that lets you do so). The container in question might look like a sign, a shopping bag, or a gift. Right-click or Apple-click it, choose Open from the floating wheel menu, and then select Copy to Inventory after the entire list of contents

General Design Advice: Semi-Human Parts

- Wings and tails are notorious for interfering with women's clothes, in particular. Because wings attach at the shoulderblades, they can interfere with the bodices of many dresses and even with camisoles. Also, bell-shaped prim skirts can overlap wingtips, and even create **occlusion** if the skirt texture is partly transparent.
- Tails are often scripted to flick or wag unpredictably, so they can make looser-fitting clothes look twitchy. Be especially mindful when trying to combine tails with flexi skirts; too much motion just confuses the eye and looks wrong.
- It is bad form to wear wings in crowded areas of Second Life, like stores and casinos, because the edges of wings are always transparent, and usually much larger than the span of the parts of wings you can see. This is a problem because the SL grid only allows you to see through transparent objects. You cannot "reach through" them with the cursor to touch, click on, or otherwise interact with something else, like an object for sale, or a chair you want to sit down on. So be good to your fellow residents and check your wings at the door, if not the entry point, long before you might interfere with someone else's plans.
- Horns and ears look best with hair that covers the place they attach, and with hair that does not match or blend with them color-wise. Horns can be especially tricky with hair that is similar or identical in length; you want your horns to look menacing or demonic, not like two especially unruly cowlicks. For that matter, ears that don't stand up much higher than the hair surrounding them can look like they are possessed, especially untamable locks of hair.

appears. This will empty the container and put all the bits and pieces of your new avatar into its own folder in your Inventory. You can then delete the container, which is a good idea as a way to keep your Inventory relatively uncluttered.

If you choose to go semi-human, spend some time with your new body in a quiet corner on a posing stand, attaching each piece one at a time. Because there's so much subtle variation in each human base avatar, your semi-human avatar parts might not fit you perfectly straight out of the vended box. This is also wise because you'll have to remember where everything attaches if you ever want to change back to simple human form. Similarly, it helps to see attachments like wings, ears, horns, and tails from all angles. This will help you know which clothes will look best while you're wearing these extra parts.

Alternative Anatomy: Going Non-Human

If two arms and two legs is still too boring, you can chuck the base human shape altogether and take on an entirely different species—familiar, fantastical, or utterly alien in every sense. Look at all these incredible options in Figures 2.25–2.28.

Copyright Storm Thunders.

FIGURE 2.25

FIGURE 2.26

FIGURE 2.27

FIGURE 2.28

How does this work? Essentially, by fooling the Second Life grid. If you open your Inventory, you will see that your avatar is still wearing a humanlike base shape. But part or all of this shape has been concealed with textures or prims scripted to be invisible. This blank slate enables designers to go beyond— way beyond—the limitations of a humanoid foundation in size, scale, and proportion.

Many of the same rules and considerations apply to nonhuman avatars as to semi-human avatars. But there is one that definitely applies to your travels and explorations if you choose to shed that human skin entirely. Some areas within Second Life are restricted to human or semi-human visitors only, mostly for role-playing reasons (i.e., if it's a Transylvanian village, logically, you'll want to go there dressed as either a sexy peasant ready to be bitten, or as a hungry vampire).

Other areas might not have explicit rules about the appearance of visitors. Most, in fact, do not. But you'll know you are wrecking the ambiance if you show up at a romantic jazz club dressed as a Purple People Eater. So do try to keep common sense, and the welfare and good humor of your fellow residents, in mind.

In the next chapter, we will cover Second Life fashion as an art form, an addiction, and the means of making a first impression. (If you think you spent a lot of time and money creating your avatar, just wait till you see how you can dress it.)

ADDITIONAL CREDITS

You can find all the brand, style, color, and designer information on items shown in the figures in the online appendix you get when registering your book at at www.peachpit.com/secondlife. See page v for details.

chapter 3

DESIGNING YOUR LOOK

There are as many ways to dress yourself in Second Life as there are in real life—in fact, probably more. Clothing vendors can be found in almost every mall and village you visit, and the variety they offer simply boggles the mind. Whether you tend toward business casual attire, period clothing, formal wear, or a little bit of everything, it's almost certain you'll be able to put together the look you want.

In this chapter, we'll examine the different types of clothing you can wear and how each clothing type is assembled. You'll also learn how to shop for the clothes and accessories that suit your personality, without falling prey to common "newbie" mistakes or buying poor quality. We will also show you how to custom-fit what you can put on your body (when possible) so your outfits don't just look good—they look good on you, too.

FIGURE 3.1 All of the garment types, by Inventory icon, in the bottom-most layer of Second Life clothes.

FIGURE 3.2 All of the garment types, by Inventory icon, in the middle layer of Second Life clothes.

FIGURE 3.3 All of the garment types, by Inventory icon, in the top-most layer of Second Life clothes.

Second Life Clothing Undone

As we discussed in Chapter 2, a Second Life avatar is assembled in *layers*. The first layer over the shape is the skin, followed by eyes and hair, and then—at last—by clothes. Clothes are also worn in successive layers on top of, or alongside, all of these body parts. From the skin on up, these layers are:

1. T-shirt, underpants, gloves, socks, the shoe base (see Figure 3.1)
2. Shirt, pants, left shoe, right shoe (see Figure 3.2)
3. Skirt, jacket (see Figure 3.3)

This variety of garment type and layer-ability is what makes Second Life clothing so customizable. Also, because clothes are created on templates in software programs, they can be partly transparent to reveal whatever is layered underneath. So some single pieces are actually combinations of various garments, cleverly designed to look like they are one (see Figure 3.4 for examples).

There are, however, a few limitations to the way Second Life clothing works:

○ You cannot change the order in which garment types are layered, i.e., a T-shirt can never go over a jacket;

○ You cannot wear more than one of the same garment types at once; for example, if you're wearing a skirt and you try to put on another, you'll just change clothes;

FIGURE 3.4 Outfits made from layering multiple garments, including tattoos and nail polish.

○ You can't turn one garment into another of a different type; for example, underpants are underpants forever, even if the item in your Inventory is modifiable.

This last item is especially important if you like wearing tattoos (commonly drawn on undershirts) or nail polish (drawn on gloves or socks). If you buy an outfit that looks especially detailed or complicated, you might have to make a choice. The choice is often obvious, though—very few outfit "parts" are optional. You usually have to wear everything the designer made as part of an outfit to make the ensemble look right.

That's how your clothing looks and functions in Second Life in the most general terms. Now that you've learned about the technical stuff, we can dive into the first part of the fun: getting dressed.

Getting Dressed

Since you have a basic understanding of what's in your virtual closet, it's time to change out of your default clothes. You probably bought some different clothes while you were out shopping for skin, hair, and other body parts. So you're ready for the big moment: trying on something new.

If (for example) you want to take off your jacket, right- or Apple-click on the jacket icon in your Inventory and select Take Off from the drop-down menu. You can also right- or Apple-click your avatar and choose Take Off > Clothes > Jacket. If you're trying to change jackets, this step isn't necessary; find an item in your Inventory, right- or Apple-click it, and choose Wear from the floating menu that appears.

The biggest catch with clothes in Second Life is the same as it is in real life— there's more to what you wear than just throwing on anything within reach. A garment can cover (or not cover you, depending on what it is) and not do its job. Clothes have to fit, they have to be appropriate, they have to be flattering, and they have to send the message you want to be sending.

Fit, Cut, and Shape

If you really want to get the most out of Second Life clothing, it helps to understand each different garment type. First, don't be too distracted by the name Linden Lab has given to each type. These real-world labels only describe the

Don't Do It!

Do *not* strip your avatar down to the skin in public places—not in a store, and never in front of other residents if you can help it. It's socially acceptable to change one piece of clothing at a time, and with practice you can accomplish switching entire ensembles without flashing anybody. But if you really have to get naked, go someplace private. Duck behind a building, go to the corner of the region you're in, or fly up in the air above 200 meters. Just get yourself out of view or other residents will think you're a newbie, or worse yet, that you're being indecent.

FIGURE 3.5 Example shirt and skirt: technically speaking, a perfect fit (no pun intended).

general layering order of Second Life clothing. Next, be aware that each garment type can serve just about any purpose in an outfit that you can imagine. SL clothes are not governed by real-world physics—they never sag, stretch, wrinkle, or otherwise lose position on the body. So the gloves garment type, for example, is often used to create sleeves, ruffles, cuffs, and other parts to a shirt, even though they are not attached to the shirt itself. It also helps to understand how the grid actually generates clothes via the in-world tools: as objects within the Second Life universe. (We'll cover this basic process in detail at the end of this chapter.) In SL, the grid actually renders a second layer of skin and presents it in sections as individual garments. So those pants, for example, are actually based on and limited by the mesh that created your avatar's legs.

Why does this matter? It affects a real-world characteristic of clothing called *drape*. In real life, your clothes are separate from your body, so they can have and hold their own shape, regardless of whatever is underneath them. In SL, however, there's no difference. So when the grid attempts to make up for the bumps, lumps, and curves of the mesh, you can end up with clothes that look completely unrealistic (see Figure 3.5). This, essentially, is the challenge involved in designing Second Life fashion: how to finesse SL's tools while they are (unfortunately) working against you.

The shirt and undershirt garment types are mainly good for making bras, corsets, camisoles, swimsuit tops, and belly shirts. Only the jacket garment type is long enough in the torso and the sleeves for anything like a blouse, a sweater, or something more modest/business casual (see Figures 3.6 and 3.7 for comparison).

FIGURE 3.6 Three different types of clothes made with the undershirt garment type.

FIGURE 3.7 Three different types of clothes made with the shirt garment type.

A true jacket, for men or for women, is a rare if not impossible find. Most blazers, sport coats, suit coats, and similar garments fit right against the body like an oddly painted second skin (see Figure 3.8 for examples).

The skirt garment type was designed to hover slightly over the hips and rear end. So the end result for Second Life skirts, no matter what, always adds an extra 20 pounds *just* where real-life women are most self-conscious. However, this same default flare in the skirt garment can make up for problems with jackets. Well-made men's suits in Second Life actually use a high-waisted, open skirt piece to make the suit coat look realistic (see Figure 3.9).

The pants garment type is just too short for jeans or trousers, ending right at the ankle to create that shrunk-it-in-the-dryer effect. The best pants designs come with additional cone- or cylinder-shaped prims to lengthen the legs appropriately (see Figure 3.10 for examples).

FIGURE 3.8 Three different types of clothes made with the jacket garment type.

FIGURE 3.9 Three different types of clothes made with the skirt garment type.

FIGURE 3.10 Three different types of clothes made with the pants garment type.

Copy/No Copy *adj.* Whether or not this object may be duplicated by its owner.

Modify/No Modify *adj.* Whether or not the object may be edited by the owner (resized, textured, recolored, or otherwise customized). Also sometimes referred to as "mod/no mod" on signage, in advertising, or in conversation.

Transfer/No Transfer *adj.* Whether or not the owner can give the object to another resident. Also sometimes referred to as "trans/no trans" on signage, in advertising, or in conversation.

Find It Fast

There are several ways to find out which items you're currently wearing; one of the easiest is to do a keyword search in your Inventory for "worn." Click the blue Inventory button at the bottom of the Second Life screen, wait for the Inventory dialog box to open, and then type the word "worn" into the Search bar of the Inventory dialog box.

Footwear in Second Life usually consists of three parts: the base, which shapes the foot, and each actual shoe, which applies straps, buckles, uppers, and heels (see Figure 3.11 for examples).

It's also important, especially with regards to clothes, to understand three characteristics of all objects in Second Life commonly known as permissions: **copy** (or **no copy**), **modify** (or **no modify**), and **transfer** (or **no transfer**).

If you're trying to put together some sort of uniform, costume, or other ensemble to be worn by more than one person, look for clothes labeled "copy/transfer." You'll be able to hold onto the original but distribute copies of it to others on your team, in your class, working in your coffeehouse, and so on.

If your avatar's shape is hard to fit, you really want to hunt for clothing that's "copy/mod," as some residents say it. This way, you can make a duplicate of what you buy and custom-tailor the copy using the Appearance tools. Then, on the off chance that you make a mistake, you still have an original.

If you need to buy clothing as a gift, make sure that the garment is transferable. It might not seem as if this particular permission is all that useful, but just wait until you see something that's perfect for your boyfriend or best friend or your other avatar. Then "trans/no trans" clothing becomes highly desirable.

FIGURE 3.11 Three different types of clothes made with the shoe and shoe base garment type.

General Design Tip: More on Clothing as Gifts

If you get your heart set on a giving a garment that's no transfer, you have two possible solutions. First, an increasing number of Second Life designers are selling gift certificates. They are often displayed and sold in their stores right alongside the merchandise, and occasionally for sale on the designer's blog or Web site. There's no social stigma involved in giving a gift certificate, either, so you can choose this option with confidence.

You might also do keyword searches for the garment or the garment's designer on the two most popular shopping Web sites for Second Life stuff: slboutique.com and slexchange.com. Both of these sites allow you to route your purchase to another resident. (There's a lot more detail on these Web sites and how to use them, later on in this chapter.)

Attachments as Accessories

Your clothes are definitely important, but any fashion consultant will tell you that accessories make or break your look. Second Life designers offer just as many accessories as clothes: scarves, jewelry, tattoos, eyeglasses, hats, boots—the list is delightfully endless.

The nicest accessories aren't made with Second Life's garment types at all. They're prim objects worn at various attachment points on your avatar's body. (Figure 3.12 shows just a handful of examples.) However, as with clothing layers, you have a limited number of these points on your avatar, and only one attachment may be worn at each point at any given time.

 **Don't Do It!**

Many skirts and dresses in Second Life are sold with pants or underpants labeled as *glitch pants*. Glitch pants are created and provided by thoughtful designers to compensate for an embarrassing fact of Second Life physics: namely, clothing panels made with flexi prims tend to fly up and stay up, when you walk or sit or touch down after flying. So if you buy an outfit or garment that comes with glitch pants, don't forget to put them on. You need them for modesty's sake or to preserve the illusion of solid fabric by covering your legs in the same color/texture as the rest of your outfit.

FIGURE 3.12 Accessories made with attachments.

FIGURE 3.13 Clothes made with attachments.

Chest
Skull
Left Shoulder
Right Shoulder
Left Hand
Right Hand
Left Foot
Right Foot
Spine
Pelvis
Mouth
Chin
Left Ear
Right Ear
Left Eyeball
Right Eyeball
Nose
R Upper Arm
R Forearm
L Upper Arm
L Forearm
Right Hip
R Upper Leg
R Lower Leg
Left Hip
L Upper Leg
L Lower Leg
Stomach
Left Pec
Right Pec

FIGURE 3.14 All 30 possible attachment points on a Second Life avatar.

Attachments are also used in some clothing designs to make up for the garment type's shortcomings or to add depth and complexity to an outfit's silhouette. Attachments are commonly worn as sleeves, skirt panels, belts, collars, ties, capes, or cloaks. Some are stationary and only move as your avatar might. Other attachments are made from flexible or "flexi" prims, which flow and sway more realistically. Figure 3.13 demonstrates how prim attachments fill out and complete various clothes and outfits.

If your avatar is human-shaped, most of your attachment points will be empty and available for whatever you want to wear. However, semi- and non-human avatars need attachments to flesh out their basic shape. So you might have tails, horns, ears, whiskers, noses, or the like taking up some of the attachment slots you'd otherwise have available (see Figure 3.14).

To put on an attachment, click the blue Inventory button. To remove an attachment, you can either right-click on the item in your Inventory folder and select Detach, or you can right-click on the item on your avatar and choose Detach from the Pie chart menu.

Unlike clothing layers, attachments can be assigned to a point other than the one chosen by the designer. With sunglasses, for example, you can simply move the attachment from your nose to elsewhere on your face. To reassign an attachment, click the blue Inventory button along the bottom of the Second Life window to open the Inventory dialog box. Right- or Apple-click on the item you want to move, choose Attach To, and select a different unused point.

If you reassign an attachment, you'll have to reposition it with the Edit tools to scoot it back into place. Don't even try to do this without a posing stand;

it's just too easy to bump or reach for the arrow keys and then your avatar will move. Most hair salons have freely available (and freely copyable) **posing stands** scattered throughout their stores, because hair almost always needs adjusting. So pay a return visit to your favorite hair boutique and look around for an available stand to use.

To reposition an attachment, click the blue Inventory button to open the Inventory dialog box. Locate the item you want to work with, right- or Apple-click it, and choose Wear from the menu that pops up. Then right-click on a posing stand and choose Stand, Pose, or Sit. (The command can vary based on how the posing stand was scripted, but it is always located in the 10 o'clock position on the Pie wheel menu.)

Once you're posed, right- or Apple-click on the attachment until you see it highlighted in yellow. Then choose Edit from the Pie chart menu. The Build dialog box will appear; click the Object tab page, which is set to Position by default. A set of two- and three-dimensional arrows in green, red, and blue will appear on the highlighted attachment (see Figure 3.15). By clicking-and-dragging one of these arrowheads, you can push or pull the attachment into place.

Next, if necessary, activate the Rotate tools by clicking the radio button just underneath Position on the Object tab page. Now the arrows will turn into rings (see Figure 3.16). By clicking and dragging on these rings, you can turn the highlighted attachment and further finesse it into just the right spot on your avatar.

ʃLanguage

posing stand *n.* A flat, usually round platform that's scripted to suspend an avatar off the ground with arms and legs extended. Posing stands are essential for sculpting an avatar's shape and for custom-fitting any sort of attachment. They are also widely available for free or the nominal price of L$, in any number of clothing stores, junkyards, and other freebie-rich locations.

⊘ **Don't Do It!**

Never attach anything to your avatar's eyes. They are scripted to blink and glance and otherwise move constantly, like your own eyes in real life, so anything linked to them will refuse to stay in place.

FIGURE 3.15 Repositioning an attachment—the Edit > Object > Position tools.

FIGURE 3.16 Repositioning an attachment—the Edit > Object > Rotate tools.

Both of these tools take a steady, delicate touch, so try not to get frustrated. It's a good idea to move the cursor off and on these tools when you're getting accustomed to them. Depending on the color of the ambient light and the texture or terrain you are working against, it can be difficult to see which tool you're selecting. But look closely, and you'll see that each arrow or ring gets slightly larger and slightly brighter after you grab it.

It's also a very good idea to check your avatar from every angle before you hop down off the posing stand. An attachment can easily look perfect from one side and way off from another. It's especially important to do this double-checking with very small or very nondescript attachments. You don't want to leave attachments accidentally tucked inside your avatar (making it very hard to grab and retrieve them) or to leave attachments hanging off the body.

➡ General Design Tip: Male Avatars and Posing Stands

Most posing stands work just fine for female avatars but not for male ones. When a guy hops on an average posing stand, his feet sink right through it, making it impossible to adjust shoes, shoe bases, pant cuffs, greaves, or anything else that needs to fit properly from the knees down. So here's a quick and easy piece of advice for the gentlemen: try out any pose stand before you take a copy or buy it. You don't want to get caught with one you can't use when you're in a hurry.

Creating Outfits

If you're a true *fashionista*, you're going to be mixing and matching all sorts of clothing pieces whether you bought them together or not. Fortunately for you, you can save such combinations as outfits, which you can take on and off with ease.

To save an outfit, put on all the clothes and other attachments you want to group together. Right- or Apple-click your avatar and choose Appearance from the Pie chart menu. The Appearance dialog box will appear. Click the Make Outfit button, and the Make New Outfit dialog box will appear (Figure 3.17).

The Make New Outfit dialog box lists every possible clothing slot and attachment point, and shows which of those slots are currently used. It also has a column for body parts—shape, skin, hair, and eyes—so you can save these options as fashion accessories, too. Click each of the check boxes next to the items you want to include in this outfit, give the outfit folder a unique name, and click Save.

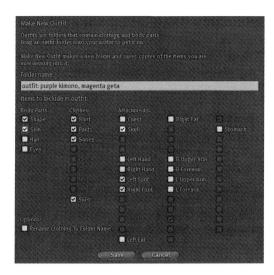

FIGURE 3.17 The Appearance > Make New Outfit dialog box.

There are a few quirks in this process, too, that you should keep in mind if you're going to use it extensively:

○ Most hair in Second Life is made up from prim attachments, which do not correspond to the Hair check box in the Make Outfit dialog box (only the bald cap "reads" as Hair). To make sure you put your entire hairstyle into an Outfit, check your Inventory first to see where the wig, bangs, braids, and so on are attached. Then click those check boxes along with the Hair check box.

○ If you wear the same shape, skin, eyes, and hair most of the time, make that combination into its own Outfit called "Basic Appearance 1" or something similarly logical. It's also not a bad idea to add in your favorite tattoo, eyelashes, facial hair, nail polish, and naughty bits, too.

○ When you create an Outfit, the folder you also create for it will appear in the Clothing folder in your Inventory. Everything you assigned to this Outfit will be moved or copied into this folder, too. But other things provided with those clothes, like landmarks, pictures, and posing stands, will not move.

○ Outfit pieces do not get priority or stay locked in place if you put on something else. For example, if you are wearing an outfit that includes a skirt and you put on another skirt, you will change clothes.

○ Making an outfit doesn't change a garment type's permissions, either. If clothing was made to be no copy, no modify, or no transfer, it will stay that way no matter where it appears in your Inventory.

Start Shopping

The logical way to begin your shopping spree is by using Search. (This is a mini-tutorial on using Second Life's Search feature; there's a far more extensive look at it in Chapter 4, "Designing Your Persona.")

Click the blue Search button along the bottom of the Second Life window to open the Search dialog box. You can narrow down the number of listings you'll be searching by clicking on one of the tab pages. Or you can choose the default All tab page, type a keyword into the Find text box, and click Search (Figure 3.18).

FIGURE 3.18 Searching for clothing in the Shopping category.

If you're looking for something specific, start out with the most common search term you can think of and see what you find. For instance, you might start with "medieval;" after that you could also try other keyword search terms like "elves," or "fairies." Also keep in mind that Search Places listings are automatically generated, but Search Classifieds listings are paid for by the advertiser. This may or may not make the store more likely to carry the item you're looking for, but it *is* more likely that that advertiser is serious about his business and that his listing is being kept somewhat up to date.

Note that classified listings are ordered by default based on how much the advertiser paid for her listing, so the businesses at the top of the default results are likely to be the bigger brand names and more popular stores. But don't shy away from some of the smaller designers who are just getting started. Many of them have a lot of talent, even if they haven't built up a large clientele just yet.

Shopping Smart

Many, *many* residents design clothing and accessories for a living in Second Life. There are hundreds—perhaps even thousands—of stores, malls, markets, and boutiques. So if you hate shopping in real life, SL is no picnic. (On the other hand, if you love it, you can probably make a killing as a personal stylist.)

There are a few considerations to keep in mind when you're out on the prowl for something nice to wear. In other online worlds, everything for sale is created and sold by the game's creators. In Second Life, almost *nothing* in-world was made by the Lindens, for sale or otherwise. The vast majority of what you see was built, and is often sold by, other residents. On the one hand, this means creativity rules the day. But on the other, there's no consistency in pricing or quality and no recourse or refunds if you buy a lemon. So caveat emptor applies: that means "buyer beware."

How to Window Shop

First, check the price. Rest the cursor on the vendor—usually a picture of the clothes you want—and wait. A small white dialog box will appear, containing the name of the item, the name of the designer, and whether or not the item is free (it will say "Free to Copy" if it is) or "For Sale" along with the price in Lindens (see Figure 3.19).

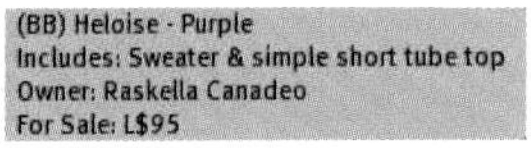

Now, figure out what you get for the price on the "tag." Right- or Apple-click on the vendor and choose Buy from the Pie menu. The Buy Contents dialog box will appear (see Figure 3.20), but don't worry. You haven't bought anything until or unless you click the Buy button.

Look at all the items listed in this dialog box very closely—expand it from left to right, too, until all the words next to the icons are displayed—and ask the following questions:

○ **Are you getting just one garment or more?** A really good deal means an entire outfit, including shoes and sometimes jewelry. Multiple copies of the same garment in many different colors, sold together as a "fat pak," are also a good find.

○ **Are the garments resizable?** Look at the information shown in parentheses after every item in the box. If you don't see the words "No Modify," then you can lower hemlines, extend sleeves, and otherwise custom-fit the garments in Appearance mode to fit your avatar exactly.

FIGURE 3.19 Just the facts: What it is, who made it, and how much it costs.

FIGURE 3.20 The Buy Contents dialog box.

○ **Is there a picture of the garment(s) included?** This is an extremely valuable extra that many designers do not provide. A picture will let you remind yourself what these clothes look like, long after you've bought other things and forgotten what's what, without having to put anything on.

○ **Is there a landmark to the store included?** Another thoughtful extra, especially if you are so caught up in shopping that you forget to make one yourself.

○ **Is a posing stand included?** A posing or pose stand is a flat object you can "stand" on in order to look at yourself from all angles using the arrow keys, and see how or if something actually fits. Every avatar needs one, but few designers actually distribute them.

The very best deal when buying clothes is anything color-changeable. These words—"color change"—tell you that these garments are scripted to turn any one of 108 colors (see Figure 3.21). You choose what color you want, and can change your mind as often as you like. This essentially means you bought over 100 outfits for the price of one, especially if you get a collection of separates.

FIGURE 3.21 The Color Change chart.

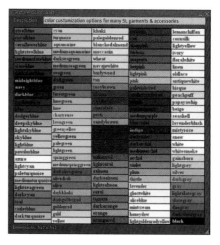

Shopping on a Budget

If you're not made of Lindens, fortunately you're in luck. Second Life is not like online games where the same thing is always the same price, and you rarely get anything for free unless you take advantage of a bug. SL's residents still largely believe in keeping things affordable (except when it comes to real estate). So there's a lot of quality, useful stuff out in the metaverse that's cheap or free for the taking. Search for **yard sales**, **junkyards**, **freebies**, or just the word "sale." These terms are all synonymous in Second Life for "finding a bargain."

Yard sales are mostly just like their real-world counterparts. Someone is getting rid of all sorts of things in their own Inventory for a reasonable price. On the plus side, yard sales are a buffet of anything and everything, and some of them are just plain enormous. Some yard sales are one-time-only events and are usually quite small. But many yard sales are actually stores, where the owners continuously buy and resell other residents' clutter. So you are likely guaranteed to find new things at the same yard sale if it's a permanent fixture and you go back on a regular basis.

On the negative side, yard sales can be a tremendous time suck. You'll spend a lot of time—a *lot* of time—looking through Search, browsing each place, and moving on with nothing. This is especially true if you're looking for something specific or if you're trying to build a wardrobe (or a living room set, or a garden full of flowers). You also have to be ready to grab what you like, because yard sales are first-come-first-served. You might find the occasional item that's selling copies of itself, but most of the time you're offered the one and only original.

Junkyards are even more disorganized and time consuming. But the quantity and variety of stuff you can find, for little or no L$, is just simply amazing. The permanent and most popular junkyards are especially jam-packed with useful stuff, and the selection is updated every week or every month. That's the plus side. Here's the downside.

Most of the time, stuff in junkyards is packaged in a cube-shaped box that's scripted to display a little floating text just overhead. This floating text is very useful; it tells you the type of item and how many different items are inside this box. But junkyards can be little more than row after row, or shelf after shelf, of these box-shaped objects. The floating text tends to overlap unless you're looking at it straight-on, then so do all the boxes, and you really have to move in close and look to see what's available.

Freebies are residents' gifts to one another, plain and simple, especially to newcomers who are still trying to get their bearings. Freebies are also widely available, not just in the bargain shops and junkyards. They are also scattered throughout Second Life in the most popular boutiques featuring the

*ſ*Language

yard sale *n.* A one-time event, or a type of store, where used goods are sold at deeply discounted prices.

junkyard *n.* A type of "store" that mainly carries items sold for L$1, items that are free to copy, or freebies.

freebie *n.* Single items or boxes of items (sometimes hundreds or thousands of them) that are available for nothing or for L$1.

FIGURE 3.22 The contents of a box of freebie clothes—lots and lots of choices.

best-designed merchandise. In part, this is still an act of generosity. Many top designers know the value of offering a really nice free gift just for stopping by, and sometimes this gift is a retired or out-of-stock design that's just as nice as what's on the shelf. Figure 3.22 shows examples of really nice freebies, just to prove they are out there and worth hunting down.

Believe it or not, there are also shopping sites for Second Life stuff on the Web (see Figures 3.23 and 3.24). That's right: outside of Second Life proper. SLBoutique (www.slboutique.com) and SLExchange (www.slexchange.com) will sell you an item for yourself or as a gift for someone else, and then deliver your purchase(s) to an avatar's Inventory in-world.

Shopping online rather than in-world can make sense for a couple reasons. First, it's easier than contending with lag, or waiting to get into Second Life if the grid is down. Also, on SLExchange, you can spend real dollars and avoid the hassle of currency exchange. Both sites offer in-world ATMs and other ways to move Lindens from your avatar's pocket into your accounts with each Web site.

Designers will sometimes mark items down for sale online, and offer slightly lower prices overall. The strategy there is usually an attempt to drive traffic to the designer's in-world shops. But, if a designer doesn't have a Second Life storefront, his or her prices on these Web sites don't have to be as high as the competition. Either way, if you want to take a quick visual sampling of what's for sale in SL, the Web sites are a faster, easier way to glance through a large quantity of goods.

General Design Advice:
Keep Your Favorite Designers in Business

Freebies are also a reliable way to give your favorite designers your customer feedback. Every time a resident grabs a copy of a free item, or pays L$1 for a nearly-free item, the designer gets an instant notification message from the grid. The overall number of freebies is a definite indication of foot traffic. Rotating free gifts to vary the style, color, or type of gift offered can also provide general information on what customers prefer. So the moral of this story is, if you like a particular store's merchandise or a certain designer's style, grab those freebies. You're getting a nice little gift and sending a message to them to keep up the good work.

FIGURE 3.23 SLBoutique—
www.slboutique.com.

FIGURE 3.24 SLExchange—
www.slexchange.com.

Examining Clothes for Quality

When you're new to Second Life and you're not a clothing designer, it can be quite difficult to spot clothes that are poorly made. It's especially challenging when you only have the vendor pictures to go on. The most exaggerated model poses can leave you wondering—how will that look on me?

Although any piece of Second Life clothing will fit on any human-shaped avatar (and quite a few semi-human ones as well), the shape of your specific SL body can cause issues. Sometimes, fabric textures will stretch as the texture is "wrapped" around the shape. Common problem areas often include the breasts, shoulders, waist, or even the legs, in the case of very tall avatars. If there's significant detailing like embroidery or stitching in those areas, the stretching will be even more noticeable.

In an ideal metaverse, you could get a demo version of an outfit to "try before you buy," just like you can with most hair, some skin, and even a few shapes. Unfortunately, this trend hasn't caught on for clothing yet, so you're still subject to caveat emptor. Generally speaking, most clothing will resize just fine with only slight variations between avatars. But if you find you're having frequent trouble, consider resculpting the parts of your avatar's shape that are warping your clothes.

Sometimes, though, the overall quality of clothing is just plain poor. A quick glance at the picture of a garment won't do the trick, either. In fact, it's often a very good idea to use the Camera Controls to zoom in for a good long look. Here's a list of telltale signs that a garment isn't as well-made as it might seem:

○ Do the seams and details match up at the shoulders, neck, sides, and waist?

○ Are there any gaps or discolored areas in the texture that don't belong there?

○ Is there a narrow band of white, or "halo," around the outline of the garment?

On the opposite side of the spectrum, a high-quality item created by a talented graphic artist will stand out in a crowd (see Figure 3.25). The most common characteristics of Second Life haute couture include:

○ Hand-drawn stitching

○ Realistically draped or folded swathes of cloth

○ Highlights, shadows, and wrinkles in the cloth that "catch the light"

○ Expertly coordinated, multiple pieces that layer transparent areas perfectly

FIGURE 3.25 The best of the best: Second Life haute couture.

Designing Clothes in Second Life

If you're out shopping and you find yourself thinking, "I could design something like that," guess what? You could be a budding Second Life clothing designer. Fortunately, SL includes in-game tools to make this easy—in fact, you already know how to use them because you've seen them in action here. The Appearance tools aren't just for tweaking your shape and making outfits. You can also use them to make brand-new clothes from scratch. All you need to make some very simple, basic SL garments are a few textures.

To demonstrate the clothing-making powers of the Appearance menu, let's work with clothing you already have: the clothing Linden Lab provides for free in the Library folder of your Inventory. We're going to apply color and use some freebie textures (also provided by Linden Lab) to make some shirts. We will play with changing the color, the texture, the dimensions, and then all these aspects mixed together—all with clothes and textures you've already got in your pocket. So let's get started.

Changing a Garment's Color

The least used freebies in Second Life are hidden in plain sight and right at your fingertips—the stuff that Linden Lab puts in your Inventory in the Library folder. We're going to work with a nice dark green shirt in the Library > Clothing folder (called, strangely enough, *Dark Green Shirt*). So go find it, put it on your avatar, and follow along to customize this garment. Figure 3.26 shows the Dark Green Shirt as it will appear when you first put it on.

FIGURE 3.26 The Dark Green Shirt, as provided by Linden Lab.

First, let's make the easiest type of change by adding color. Open the Appearance dialog box by right- or Apple-clicking on your avatar and choosing Appearance from the Pie menu. Now click the Shirt tab, and various customizing options will appear toward the right side of the screen, including the Color/Tint window (see Figure 3.27).

Click inside the Color/Tint window, and the Color Picker dialog box will appear. We are going to lay colors over the top of the crushed velvety-looking texture used in this shirt, and this combination will tint the shirt. As you can see in Figure 3.28, there are many ways to choose color, including a group of presets in a double horizontal row near the bottom edge of the dialog box.

Start by clicking the Apply Immediately check box so the colors you choose will appear right away. Now choose colors at random, study the difference each one makes, and click the blue Revert button to undo. You can select from the presets, or click on the square eyedropper tool and use the crosshairs to navigate the rainbow-hued box. If you choose colors that are paler than the dark green texture, you will still be able to see the crumpled surface underneath and the change might be quite subtle. If you choose a color that's darker than the texture, though, the shirt will turn completely solid.

A Word on Advanced Clothing Design Techniques

We've said it before: This book is *not* a how-to-do-it-all sort of technical manual. So if you're set on making Second Life haute couture, you should be ready to invest some fairly serious time learning the more advanced methods.

The most successful and idolized clothing designers in SL use Adobe Photoshop or Corel Paint Shop Pro New to create their own textures. These designers also use a specific set of clothing templates, which give designers much more control over exactly how a garment looks. It takes time, effort, and discipline to master these aspects of SL clothing design. So be prepared to make that investment.

If you still want to learn more, above and beyond the following very, *very* simple techniques covered in this chapter, start with Linden Lab's introductory materials. In your Inventory, there's a note card in the Library > Clothing folder called *Creating Avatar Clothing*, which provides some useful general advice on developing clothes in Photoshop. There's also a folder full of templates in Library > Textures called *Avatar Body and Clothing Templates*. These resources are easy to find, free of charge, and they'll help you figure out how deeply involved you want to get.

Additionally, you can take an in-world class, visit the forums, *and* pore over the Knowledge Base. You've got a lot to learn, and a lot of practice time ahead. But there's always room in SL for the next great clothing designer, so it just might be worth it.

Also, notice that the numbers in the R, G, and B value text boxes change every time you switch colors. Each color in Second Life is made up of a mixture of different amounts of red (R), blue (B), and green (G), with zero being the least amount and 255 being the most. This is how the color of the Dark Green Shirt was adjusted in Figure 3.29. If you go to the online appendix and look up this figure, you'll see three color "recipes" made up from three numbers. Notating colors as sets of numbers in this manner is a quick, easy, and foolproof way to make sure you get the exact shade or hue you're seeking.

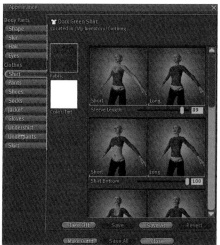

FIGURE 3.28 The Color Picker dialog box.

FIGURE 3.27 The Shirt tab page in the Appearance dialog box.

FIGURE 3.29 The Dark Green Shirt with three different colors applied to it.

FIGURE 3.30 The Pick Texture dialog box, with the default Dark Green Shirt fabric texture in view.

FIGURE 3.31 The Dark Green Shirt with three different textures applied.

Changing a Garment's Texture

Now let's experiment with texture. Return the Color/Tint setting to white (i.e., no extra color) by typing 255 in each of the RGB value windows. Next, click inside the Fabric window, and the Pick Texture dialog box will appear (see Figure 3.30).

Everything that appears in this window, no matter where it's stored or what it's called, can be applied to clothing. To demonstrate the flexibility of textures, all of the ones used in Figure 3.31 are not actually described as cloth. Yet these shirts look interesting and have great possibilities, and you'd never know what textures were used to create them unless you read their file names.

Changing a Garment's Shape

Finally, let's take virtual scissors, needle, and thread to this shirt and change its shape. There are seven ways to cut, shorten, lengthen, and otherwise custom-fit this shirt. Use the scrollbar running down the right side of the Appearance dialog box and move any of the slider bars to start tweaking.

You can adjust these settings two ways: by clicking-and-dragging the slider bars, or by changing the number values. Figure 3.32 shows the Dark Green Shirt customized differently, along with the numerical values of all seven settings, so you can duplicate these looks if you want.

Transforming an Entire Garment

Now let's take all these possibilities and really remake that Dark Green Shirt. Here are six essentially new shirts, all created by using the entirely free and customizable Dark Green Shirt, free textures of all sorts, various colors, and the relevant Appearance tools (see Figure 3.33).

FIGURE 3.32 The Dark Green Shirt customized—from left to right, a simple crewneck T-shirt, a muscle shirt-type tank top, and a relatively modest peasant blouse.

FIGURE 3.33 The Dark Green Shirt transformed—top row, from left to right, a bustier; a modest peasant blouse; a bikini top. Bottom row, from left to right: a cap-sleeve T-shirt; a flamenco top, and a turtleneck sweater.

Now that your avatar is all kitted out, it's time to ease into Second Life society. The next chapter is called "Designing Your Persona." It covers the importance of your Profile, more ways to use Search, and how the two are interconnected.

ADDITIONAL CREDITS

You can find all the brand, style, color, and designer information on items shown in the figures in the online appendix you get when registering your book at at www.peachpit.com/secondlife. See page v for details.

chapter 4

2nd Life | Web | Interests | Picks | Classified | 1st Life | My Notes

Name: **Rachel Darling**

Photo:

Born:
6/2/2006

Account:
Resident
Payment Info Used

Partner: ⑦

Ratings:
Behavior	+6
Appearance	+6
Building	+4
Given	+3

Groups:
Member of Avilion Order
Member of Builders of Ketora
Member of Darling Isobel

DESIGNING YOUR PERSONA

4

Right now, as these words are sitting on the page, the total population of Second Life is fast approaching 8 million residents. So it's easier than ever to bump into strangers and start a casual conversation. But in some ways, it's more and more of a challenge to make friends.

In this chapter, you will learn how to add the next layer of personality to your avatar and online life, so you will be and feel more approachable. You'll learn how to create a Profile for yourself that will invite other people to talk to you, and how to spot the stuff of small talk and commonalities in others' Profiles. You'll take a good, long look at the single most useful tool in every dimension of Second Life—and that tool is Search. Finally, you'll learn how to combine what you put into your Profile with Search results to find entrées into the areas of SL that match your interests.

name *n.* Also known as *nameplate*, *title*, and *titler*, it's not just the combination of first and last names you choose when you register. Also the oval-ish semitransparent area hanging over an avatar's head when you're in-world, which displays his or her name. Sometimes, there is also a second line of text positioned over an avatar's name; this is his or her active title. (Titles are assigned by leaders of Groups, and you only receive a title after you join a Group. We will cover Groups in more detail later on in this chapter.)

Advertise Yourself: Creating Your Profile

You can make a first impression in Second Life by walking past another resident. Or, alternatively, you can make a first impression via your Profile, which is a set of biographical "pages" provided to every resident of Second Life. Your Profile can, and does, reveal a great deal about your personality, your interests, your credibility, and even your general air of friendliness.

If you want to look at your own Profile, or the Profile of somebody standing nearby your avatar, click on the semitransparent oval hanging over his or her head. This will open the semitransparent pie menu, and the Profile option is at the center right.

Looking at others' Profiles when they're not standing nearby requires a different strategy. The easiest way to find a Profile is to find the resident by name using Search. Click the blue Search button along the bottom of the Second Life window; then click the People tab and type the name of the resident into the blank text box near the upper left corner. (We will explore Search much more thoroughly later in this chapter.)

There are six pages to your Profile, each devoted to a specific type of information. The actual use for these pages, though, continues to evolve just as Second Life keeps growing and changing. So let's have a look at each part of the Profile in turn, starting with the default first page, 2nd Life.

Your Profile: The 2nd Life Page

There are nine text boxes and other such areas on the 2nd Life tab page, along with half a dozen blue buttons at the bottom edge. Some of these areas are filled in automatically by the Second Life server, i.e., the contents of these text

A Blank Profile Tells Other People That...

- You are a rank newbie beginner with no idea what you're doing.
- You are antisocial and don't want to interact with others.
- Your avatar is not your "real" one, and therefore you are trying to skulk around anonymously and make a nuisance of yourself. This assumption is especially likely if you are a new resident *and* your payment information is not on file.

boxes cannot be customized. The Name box, for example, is going to display the avatar's name; the Born box shows the date that avatar was created; the Account box reveals whether or not the avatar's account is free or paid and if that resident's payment information is on record (see Figure 4.1).

FIGURE 4.1 The 2nd Life tab page of the Profile.

Do *not* click on any part of an avatar to get to the Profile, even your own. If you click on yourself, you could detach something crucial, such as your hair, your jewelry, or even part of your clothes. Also, don't forget about those indiscreet naughty bits, which will "yell" something explicit or embarrassing if you click them by accident. These bits can (and often are) located on an avatar's lips, feet, or tail, in addition to other obvious places, such as the chest, the groin, and the rear end.

The most important areas on this tab page of your Profile—in terms of conveying biographical info about yourself—are the Photo, the Groups list, and the About: Text box. These are the three places someone else will glance over first, because residents have control over what appears here, so this information is unique. Also, the quality and presentation of this information, specifically, can persuade someone to dig deeper into your Profile.

The Photo area is the place to drag-and-drop in an image of your avatar. It's usually a "pic" that's taken in-world, using a combination of poses or animations, the Snapshot tool, and the Camera Controls. The final product (if you like it and decide to keep it) is saved to either your computer's desktop, or to the Photo Album folder in your Inventory.

Second Class in Second Life?

TO PAY FOR your Second Life account, or not to pay for Your Second Life account—is money the real question? No. Ultimately, it's trustworthiness. If you are willing to upgrade from a free Basic account to a paid Premium account, and put your personal details on file with Linden Lab, then you will be judged more positively. Linden Lab will be happier to have you around, and so will other residents.

This situation did not always exist. Back in the days when Second Life was a smallish community of thousands, free Basic membership wasn't necessarily a detriment. As a marketing strategy, obviously, it has served Linden Lab very well to allow curious people to try SL without making a commitment. But now SL is exploding, both in population and notoriety. Basic membership used to be a big selling point, a far better way to try a virtual world than time-limited trialware or feature-limited crippleware. Now it's become an easy way for troublemakers to access the grid with speed and relative anonymity. In fact, the increasingly common sentiment about Basic members is that they are griefers, hackers, and other people who don't want to be held accountable for their actions, until proven otherwise.

Linden Lab has acknowledged this shift in perspective, and they've added new features in response. If you own a small island (a private SIM), you can set your security tools to automatically deny entrance to avatars without payment information on file. Also, some locations/destinations will advertise their unavailability to unpaid residents,

as a signal to "legitimate" residents who seek grief-free places where they can spend their time. So if you are using a Basic account to have a free look-see, while you're trying to decide whether or not to join Second Life, your tour might be restricted. You really have to pay for a Premium account to be able to go anywhere and see everything.

However, there's an additional wrinkle in this situation, which is wholly technical. Linden Lab used to say its current server setup would support a maximum of 30,000 residents in-world at the same time. Now they cite the maximum to be 40,000. At this writing, it's possible for a few thousand extra residents to sneak in, but server performance suffers badly. Lag becomes persistent, and residents who can get in-world are more likely to crash. It's also logical to assume that the longer this situation lasts, the fewer people will try to get online when the online population is at or over maximum. They've learned that the hassle isn't worth it.

Critics and tech-types have speculated that restricting unpaid residents to one part of the Second Life world would be a logical short-term solution. But the potential social consequences of such an action are already, also, widely publicized. If Linden adopts this strategy, they will formalize the growing underclass, and sabotage their well-advertised, egalitarian credo. Indeed, universal unrestricted access is a key feature that makes SL unique among other virtual worlds. If that changes or gets taken away, SL will become a little more disappointingly similar to the competition.

➡ General Design Advice: Profile Portraits

If you have a graphics program such as Adobe Photoshop or Corel Paint Shop Pro, save your self-portrait to your desktop and crop it. However, the ideal size for a Profile Photo is 256 by 512 pixels—a much smaller finished product than the file you'll create. It really does take a certain eye to compose or filter out what won't end up in the finished Photo while you're snapping the full-screen image. So if you want a really nice photo for your profile, find a good portraitist or photographer and pay a few Lindens to get a professional's help.

Here are some nicely composed, well-proportioned Profile Photos (Figures 4.2–4.4).

The Groups text box just beneath the Photo is a scrollable list of all the Groups you've joined. Although you can belong to 25 groups, the Profile page lists them alphabetically and only the first three appear in this window. Still, whatever appears in your Groups window will provide a glimpse into your hobbies and interests, and may open (or close) doors for you socially.

Some role-playing communities require a "record" of association with or proven interest in the game, world, or novels upon which their RP is based. This requirement guarantees a basic degree of familiarity with the culture and the rules, so everybody who is playing along will know what they are doing and why. Also, landlords often carefully screen the Profiles of Second Life residents who want to rent property. If a would-be tenant belongs to a Group known to attract **griefers**, or whose members are wannabe hackers, a landlord may think twice about inviting that kind of mayhem onto his or her private property.

Group membership also serves many practical purposes because of the way the Second Life grid works. For example, many designers and businesspeople in SL use Groups to make announcements to customers, affiliates, and other

ʃLanguage

griefer *n.* An avatar (a resident, really) that deliberately causes distraction or disruption inside Second Life. Griefers can be simply annoying by following someone around, by streaking in PG-rated areas, or by refusing to follow role-playing rules. But griefers can also cause serious chaos by using scripted objects that attack or disable the Second Life grid. Lindens don't like them (obviously), and neither do most residents, so this is one pastime you might want to pass up.

FIGURE 4.2 An eye-catching pose...

FIGURE 4.3 ...just enough detail in the clothing and hair...

FIGURE 4.4 ...and focus on the face.

terraform *v.* To change the
relative height of land compared to the relative height
of water, in order to create
topographical features such
as lakes, rivers, hills, mountains, etc.

interested parties—you can send a single IM to everybody belonging to a group
or hold a collective discussion without anyone else overhearing. Group membership may also limit access and activities on a particular bit of land. You can
use Group-related settings to keep strangers out of your home, to prevent non-
members from leaving trash on your lawn, and even to allow or deny someone
else the ability to build on or terraform your property.

Similarly, doors may be scripted to keep out everybody who does not belong to
that household's Group. These are other, significant reasons why someone else
might browse the Groups list on your Profile. Sometimes, the Groups to which
you do or do not belong have a lot to say about the people you trust or the people who trust you.

The third all-important area on the 2nd Life tab page is the About: Text box.
What's the most intriguing, descriptive, or crucial thing about you that you
want others to know? This is the place to spell that out—not in 500 characters
or less, but actually four lines or less. The About: Text box may be scrollable,
but it's a lot like a Web page. If you don't grab somebody with the first "bite" of
information you provide, without them having to click-and-drag that scrollbar,
chances are good they won't bother to read the rest.

So use the About: Text box to summarize the meaning of your avatar's Second
Life. List your business, praise your friends, declare your love, spell out expectations. You can expand on all these things in subsequent Profile pages, but this
area is where you are guaranteed to get one point across.

Your Profile: The Web and Interest Pages

Now that the Web tab page is working, more and more Second Life residents are
using this page to promote Second Life resources on the Web at large. Designers
have created blogs to announce the debut of new products and Web sites to promote their entire product lines. Landlords, real estate agents, and other residents who buy, sell, or rent land will use a Web site to list all their properties.
Groups with a "dual-world purpose," such as the organizers and participants
in the Second Life Community Conferences, use a mix of in- and real-world
resources to keep vital information circulating. So the Web tab page on someone's profile is worth a quick glance, just in case there's something interesting
at that URL that you don't want to miss (see Figure 4.5).

FIGURE 4.5 The Web tab page of your Profile.

The Interests tab page, to be honest, just isn't that interesting. If you want to demonstrate that you're into building, or that you have talent as a builder (just as one example), you'll get far more mileage out of dedicating a few Picks to your projects than by clicking a box or two on this page. So feel free to use the text boxes only, and type in something like, "See my Picks." This sort of quick note will drive people to the next tab page in your Profile, the second most important area, your Picks.

Your Profile: The Picks Page

By now, you might have realized that your Second Life Profile is comparable to your personal Web site in real life. (Well done! You're very perceptive!) So if that comparison holds true, you've come to the equivalent of the "Links" page: your in-world Picks.

You can list anything in your Picks—your favorite stores, shout-outs to your favorite people, information about your Second Life business, and more (see Figure 4.6 on the next page). But you only get a maximum of 10 Picks per Profile, and there are limits as to how much text will be displayed. So here are some tips on how to use Picks to their best advantage.

FIGURE 4.6 The Picks page of your Profile.

Your Picks are composed of a Photo, a short title, body text, and a **landmark**.

If you want to create a Pick of your favorite place, your home, your store, or any other Second Life location, just go there. Then open your Profile, click on the Picks tab, and click the New button near the top of the Profile dialog box. A new Picks page will automatically appear, with default text and a default Photo, prepared and uploaded by the landowner.

You can edit every part of a Picks page. If you want to add a different Photo, open your Inventory and click and drag the texture or snapshot you want into the Photo box. To change the side tab text, click once in the narrow text box just below the Photo and then start typing. The side tab text will transform once you press Enter or Return. The same basic strategy works for changing the body text; click once in the big text box, delete or add new text as you wish, and press Return or Enter to save your changes.

The general size and composition of a Picks Photo should be the same as the portrait Photo on the first page of your Profile. But there are specific considerations to keep in mind for Picks text. At most, the side tab text that will be visible when the Picks are all closed is 18 characters. Also, even though the max length of the body text is 500 characters, only six lines of text will appear without scrolling down. So try to keep your title and description of each Pick within these shorter, smaller limits.

If you're trying to arrange your Picks in a particular way, you have to trick the grid. The default order will be alphabetical, based on the first letter of the side tab text. However, you can use numbers, or an increasing number of colons (:) or exclamation points (!), to force a rearrangement. Popular reasons for doing this have to do with ranking, role-playing, or creating a chronology. But also, because your Picks are ultimately just like your favorite links or bookmarks in your Web browser, you should have control over the order in which other people will browse them.

If you own a store, a casino, a club, a garden, or any other sort of destination that needs advertising, you can use this same strategy to push yourself to the top of other people's Picks, too. To create or modify the default Picks-related information, choose About Land from the pie menu and then look at the General tab page. The way you type the name of your land in the Name text box is how it will appear whenever somebody makes a Pick. So take advantage of the side tab text defaults and begin the name of your land with colons or exclamation points.

Your Profile: The Classified Page

Just about everybody in Second Life, at one time or another, has an event, a business, or something for sale that they want to advertise. Hence, the Classified tab (see Figure 4.7 on the next page). Each Classified listing you create on this page, much the same way you create a Pick listing, appears in SL's worldwide Search. Where, when, and how these listings appear—and how effective they are—depends on how you create them.

Just like Picks, you can create a maximum of 10 Classified listings. The main components of a Classified listing are the Photo, a short title, the body text, and a landmark. However, unlike Picks, each Classified you create here serves double duty—it places an ad in Search, and it is visible to anybody viewing your profile, minus a few key bits of information at the bottom of the Classified tab page, which only you can see. So Classified listings in your Profile act as a second directory of your favorite things.

After you've written the title and added body text along with a Photo, walk to the place where you want respondents to arrive and click the Set Location button. This will create the Classified's landmark.

Don't Do It!

Do *not* use your Picks tab pages to advertise your own store, casino, club, property for sale or for rent, or other business. Some residents do; this organizational strategy seems to be left over from an earlier time in SL history when Classifieds were, perhaps, not visible in the Profile. But now, they are. So optimize your limited space. Use Picks tab pages to call attention to people, events, locations, and other important things that don't need advertising. Use the Classifieds tab pages for places, events, businesses, and locations that do.

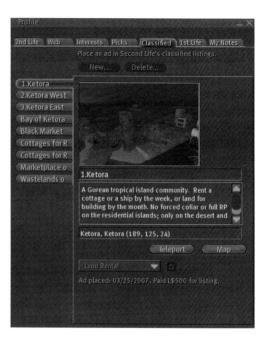

FIGURE 4.7 The Classified page of your Profile.

Now you are ready to Publish your Classified. Choose the best category for your Classified from the drop-down menu. (There might not be an exact match, but pick the best one possible.) Then check the Mature box to maximize the ad's exposure, even if the content is not R-rated. Click the blue Publish button and decide how much you want to pay, in Lindens, each real-life week, for your Classified listing. It's almost always best to check the Auto-Renew box, even if you are only offering an item or two for sale. You can always revisit your Classified listings and update or cancel them, but it's a pain in the neck to rewrite and re-list them every week.

There are two strategies to consider here. On the one hand, Second Life residents are becoming more and more savvy about using the Search tool to its best advantage, so chances are good that they will find your listing by keyword search if you provide a thorough list of keywords to work with. Then again, the more Lindens you pay for your Classified listing, the greater the chance it will appear at the top of any general search list in its category.

The best way to figure out if it's worth the cost to aim for the top of the list is to do your research. Open Search yourself and start browsing the categories of listings while pretending to be the type of customer you want to attract. Not only will this help you figure out where to put your own Classified, but it will also give you an idea of how much other people in your line of work, or selling what you have to sell, have shelled out to get top billing. (You must click OK after creating a Classified listing, or the listing will not be uploaded and saved.)

There's another way to advertise if you own the land underneath your business: by customizing certain Land Options settings. If you do these customizations, Search will "grab" text and other information from the Land Options settings and compile a listing for Search > Places. This type of promotion is less expensive than placing a Classified, but it's also more simple and limited. To use the Land Options settings for advertising, click on any part of your land—on the ground itself, not on something sitting on the land—and choose About Land from the pie menu. The About Land dialog box will appear (see Figure 4.8).

First, look at the Name and Description text boxes at the top of the General tab page. The text you type into the Name box will be the title of the Search > Places listing. The text you type into the Description text box will appear as the details in the listing.

Next, click the Options tab, and look for the Land Options settings in the middle area of this tab page (see Figure 4.9). Check the box labeled "Show in Search > Places" and drag and drop a Photo of the destination into the Snapshot box. You should also select a Search subcategory from the drop-down menu; the most practical is the default "Any Category," however.

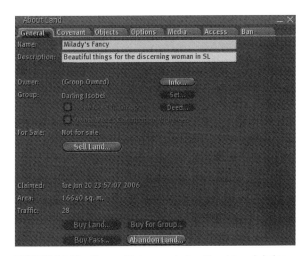

FIGURE 4.8 The General tab page in the About Land dialog box.

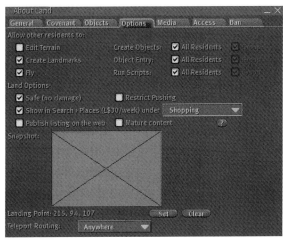

FIGURE 4.9 The Options tab page in the About Land dialog box.

The benefit in creating a Search listing this way is definitely the price. As shown, this listing costs a mere L$30 per week, and is renewed automatically as long as you own the land. There are two downsides, though. First, you can't track the success of this type of ad like you can with proper Classified listings. Second, the Description text provided here can only be a maximum of 130 characters long, compared to 500 characters in a Classified ad. So you really have to think cleverly and boil down the essence of what you want to say in order to get this type of listing to work.

Your Profile: The 1st Life and My Notes Pages

The last two pages of your Profile are entirely optional, not often visited (because they are most often left blank), and not often used (because, well, they are most often left blank.)

It's obvious why many residents leave the 1st Life page empty; everybody spends quite a bit of time, energy, and forethought creating an alternate identity, so, referencing your first life can feel somewhat counterproductive. Also, because this is still the Internet, privacy and anonymity remain precious. So don't be disappointed or put off if somebody's 1st Life page is completely bare (see Figure 4.10).

The My Notes page is, as described, intended as an easy-access place for your own notes on a particular person or avatar (see Figure 4.11). (It's definitely easier to jump to this spot than, say, comb the average overbloated Inventory for a single notecard.) But in reality, you just won't see that many avatars frequently enough to make this Notes page a viable place to keep personal notes.

FIGURE 4.10 The 1st Life page of your Profile.

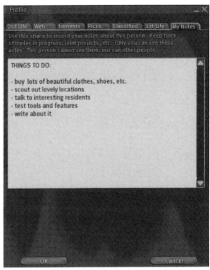

FIGURE 4.11 The My Notes page of your Profile.

Two unexpected, but interesting and practical uses for the My Notes page were uncovered during research for this book. The first, most universal application serves as a to-do list. Some Second Life business owners will use the My Notes page as a low-tech sort of appointment book/reminder list. But, they do this in their own Profile and only for themselves.

The other possible, though infrequent, use for this page is as a virtual role-playing character sheet. Traditional, pencil-and-paper-type role-players have co-opted the My Notes page as a place to paste in their SL character's stats, race and alignment information, and the contents of their all-important "knapsack." This keeps such info readily at the fingertips, where it can also be easily updated or modified. No eraser or Inventory hunting required.

Finding Your Niche: Using Search

Now that you've created numerous ways for other residents to learn about you, you might want to start learning more about other residents. The easiest, fastest, and most exponentially educational way to do this is to use Search (see Figure 4.12 on the next page).

FIGURE 4.12 The top tab, or All page, of the Search dialog box.

As already mentioned, the basic functionality of Second Life's Search feature is very similar to any search engine on the Web at large. The All tab page is especially like this—use the blank Find text box near the upper-left corner of this page to type in any keyword. Then click the blue Search button beside it on the right, and anything matching your request will scroll into the results window on the left below.

If you're doing a Search for something popular, like a casino, or if you're using very general words like *cars* or *shoes,* you'll be flooded by a tidal wave of results. Also, it's quite likely that the top 25 results (the maximum number you can see in the Search window at once) will not relate to your chosen keyword. So how do you refine the process and zero in on what you really want to find?

At this writing, there's no advanced Search capability within Second Life. Also, Linden does not police Search listings to prevent keyword incursion—adding popular keywords like *sex* to a totally unrelated ad, just so your listing will come up more frequently. Furthermore, you can't refine an SL Search using Boolean logic, the functionality that lets you use *and, or, not,* and the like to exclude keywords elsewhere on the Internet. You can use more than one word together, such as *racing cars* or *women's shoes,* and have some success. Still, your best bet is to use the other tab pages in Search as a means of narrowing down results.

Using Search: The Classifieds Page

Every time you write a Classified, this is the first place somebody else will go looking for it (see Figure 4.13).

FIGURE 4.13 The Classifieds tab page in the Search dialog box.

This is the other side of the Classified listings you create using your Profile—where everybody goes to search for things you just might want them to find. As you might assume, the categories listed in the drop-down menu are the same: Any Category, Shopping, Land Rental, Property Rental, Special Attraction, New Products, Employment, Wanted, Service, and Personal.

What actually ends up in these categories? Good question.

○ **Any Category:** The catch-all Classified page, very similar to the All tab page in Search as a whole. Keyword searches in this tab page will bring you results culled from all the other categories, for better and for worse.

- **Shopping:** Just what it says—the place to keyword-window-shop for anything you can put into Inventory. This does mean everything—shapes, skins, delicate tiny piercings, entire houses, scripts, HUD attachments… anything that the grid perceives to be an object.

- **Land Rental:** Not quite what it says. Here you'll find listings for (primarily) empty land to buy, rent, lease, or sublet by the week or month. All types of land are listed here, from Linden-owned mainland lots to lots on privately owned island SIMs. All sizes of lots are listed here, too, from 512 sq/meters on up to whole islands and (theoretically) beyond.

- **Property Rental:** Not quite what it says, either. Property usually means land plus something already constructed on it, like a house, a store, a display-type parking spot for your car, or a marina-type slip for your boat. Again, property can be for sale, rent, lease, or sublet, either by the week or by the month.

- **Special Attraction:** A totally subjective category. It's anybody's guess what belongs in here, or what can be found here, either. A quick survey of listings in this category included ads for surfing beaches, blues clubs, and gaming destinations.

- **New Products:** Another totally subjective category, filled with miscellaneous and random listings. This seems to be a place where SL merchants list new styles of existing products, rather than brand-new, never-before-seen creations.

- **Employment:** All sorts of activities relating to making Lindens and occasionally real life money. Jobs can be found here, both short- and long-term, but also ads by job banks and talent agencies, and places with camping chairs that want you to come boost their stats for them. Read these listings carefully for the fine print, and remember to scroll all the way down.

- **Wanted:** Also just what it says: if somebody wants something, they'll put a listing here. Real example: wanted listings include yard sale owners seeking used furniture; role-playing communities looking for players; residents looking for specific products that have been discontinued by particular designers; singles looking for dates, one-night stands, or partners.

- **Service:** Not just for prostitutes anymore! Real example Service listings include banks and stock exchange firms looking for investors; DJs and real life musicians looking for gigs; gardens and rental halls offering space for weddings; and real estate firms offering to find or sell land as brokers. (Okay, this is still the place to find escorts, too.)

○ **Personal:** Also not just for... well, yes, you can find escorts here as well. But also people advertising support groups, book clubs, film societies, and listing traditional newspaper-type personal ads.

Using Search: The Events Page

It would seem logical that this page in Search is the place to look for something to do. To a certain extent, this is correct. But the Events page has also become the place where businesses, designers, casinos, land developers, and other not-quite-social groups will make announcements (see Figure 4.14).

FIGURE 4.14 The Events tab page in the Search dialog box.

The categories listed in this page's pull-down menu are All, Discussion, Sports, Live Music, Commercial, Nightlife/Entertainment, Games/Contests, Pageants, Education, Arts and Culture, Charity/Support Groups, and Miscellaneous. The All tab page in Events is a good place to get a hearty sampling of what's available, and a good place to look for examples of how to write your own Events listing. But if you're interested in finding things to do, especially if you have a few days or a few weeks to plan ahead, use the more specific category settings to fill in your social calendar.

Here's the lowdown:

○ **All:** Everything ongoing and soon to get going. Events on this page are listed chronologically, albeit with a twist. The default search-for-everything setting is toggled with Ongoing and Starting Soon enabled (as opposed to searching by RL date). This results in Events at the top of the list, i.e., everything showing on the first results page, to be about an hour and a half old. If you want to find an Event starting anytime close to the actual time you're searching, skip right to the next page.

○ **Discussion:** Just what it sounds like, no holds barred in terms of topic. Real example discussions scheduled here included politics, religion, marriage, BDSM, current events, and progressive causes as the subjects *du jour*.

○ **Sports:** An intriguing mix of in-world, golden-oldie type competitions (sword fights, boxing matches, pirate battles, etc.) with hybrid offerings, like guided spinning classes for people with PCs next to their real-world exercise bikes. Also the place to bet on real-world sports events.

○ **Live Music:** Also a mix category. Approximately half in half, with live DJs spinning recorded tracks on the one hand, and live bands or solo artists performing in real time. Very diverse offerings.

○ **Commercial:** Themed sales, grand opening sales, liquidation sales, seasonal sales. Did we mention the stuff for sale? (Take your time if you want to spot anything like a real bargain.)

○ **Nightlife/Entertainment:** Just about every possible way to advertise topless and wet T-shirt contests. (Again, take your time if you want to find anything else aside from "gee-your-pixels-look-good" type Events.)

○ **Games/Contests:** Variations on the wet T-shirt theme, with ads for casinos and other perpetual SL games like Slingo, plus the occasional trivia night competition.

○ **Pageants:** Where "Best Arrangement of Pixels" type contests should be listed, but aren't. An underused and mostly empty category listing.

○ **Education:** A bounty of opportunities, with classes for every possible in-world building and scripting project, plus all sorts of real-world seminars on meaty topics such as quantum physics, financial investment, tarot and astrology, and even English as a Second Language (ESL).

○ **Arts and Culture:** Everything creative, quirky, and ambitious. In-world gallery showings of works by real-world painters and photographers. Tours of whole-environment builds, designed to be as close to performance art as possible. Even group bedtime stories, poetry readings, and psychic consultations.

○ **Charity/Support Groups:** Also a place to find support for life challenges, such as addiction, chronic pain, and depression. But, in addition, there are announcements for in-world Events raising real money for real nonprofit and charitable causes.

○ **Miscellaneous:** Browsing this category is a fun Event in and of itself.

To list your own event, click the blue Create Event button near the lower-right corner of the Events tab page. You'll be directed to the Second Life Web site's Events area and the Add Event forms page (see Figure 4.15). (Read the rules and requirements and check "I Agree" to get to the form.)

FIGURE 4.15 The Add Event form page on the Second Life Web site.

There are two bits of information you should figure out first before you try to create an Event listing. One, be sure you know what time your Event will begin and end in LST, or Linden Standard Time. This is *not* the same as GMT—it is the same as Pacific Standard Time, in California, where Linden Lab is located.

Also, scout out your Event location first. If you have land, and a house or event space of your own, no problem. But if you're new, if you still have a freebie account, or if you don't have enough space or the proper kind of venue, you'll need to host someplace else.

Using Search: The Popular Places Page

What's hot in Second Life at this very moment? What's listed on this page are the top 20 most popular places in-world, as measured by traffic stats (see Figure 4.16).

Here's the irony with reaching Popularity: many would-be visitors will be put off by that thumbs-up icon. Why? First, the default maximum occupancy for any location is 40 avatars (and, many land- or location-owners don't know how to change that setting). Therefore, Popular destinations are often too crowded to visit; the server won't let you teleport there.

FIGURE 4.16 The Popular Places tab page in the Search dialog box (search results for something PG-rated).

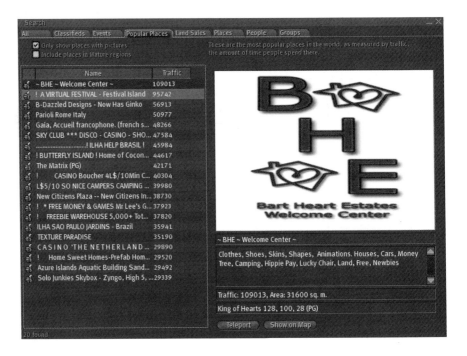

Traffic vs. Hits: Measuring Popularity

IF YOU'RE TRYING TO MAKE MONEY, or finagle your Second Life location onto this page in Search, you probably dream about traffic stats. But what does it mean when an in-world destination pops up at the top of the Popular Places page? What data is actually measured by those incredible four- and five-digit numbers, anyway?

Linden Lab provides a rather coy answer to this question near the upper-right corner of the Popular Places window. Their official statement reads, "these are the most popular places in the world, as measured by traffic, the amount of time people spend there." So in-world traffic is *not*, repeat, *not* the same thing as hits on a Web site. You will not get 134,000 unique visitors to your casino in one day. The grid can't handle it, and there aren't even enough residents logged in at any given moment to make that happen.

So what does one point of "traffic" actually equal? It equals one five-minute block of continuous time spent by one avatar in one location. Think about that. You still have to have lots and lots of people visiting your destination to make it a Popular Place. But more importantly, those people have to spend lots and lots of *time* at your destination. So measuring the number of individual residents who visit your place is not the key issue. It's measuring the average duration of each resident's visit, which provides insight into why, when, and how residents are using your location.

This, ultimately, is the reason why gaming parlors, sex clubs, and shopping malls have high traffic stats. They all give residents the same thing to do: bring an avatar to one location and hang around. This is also, ultimately, the reason why some real world businesses have failed in their attempts to establish a Second Life presence. Real life businesses are most likely using strategies and expectations set by Web site users, or in-store customers. This quantity-first mindset won't cut it with SL residents. The key to a successful and truly popular SL destination is more about quality.

So how does traffic and popularity translate into relevant usability information? Briefly, it doesn't— so whoever figures out how to import or duplicate something like a Web site cookie is going to be a hero.

Also, even if the "host" of a Popular destination is savvy enough to up that max occupancy setting, crowds are notorious for creating lag. Lag, if you remember, happens when the grid is overworked and cannot render objects fast enough to allow for "natural" movement. And frankly, there are few more frustrating experiences in Second Life than finally getting *to* a door, but literally not being able to get *through* it.

If you are bound and determined to visit a Popular Place yourself, here's a time-tested tip to help you out. Once you get to the location, step to the side, just a few paces away from the entry point, and use Mouselook and the Camera Controls to poke around (see Figure 4.17).

FIGURE 4.17 The Camera Controls palette.

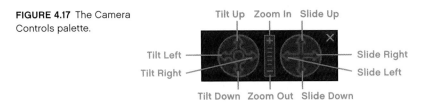

You can quickly move between first and third person with the Mouselook setting (press Escape and then M to "jump" into your avatar's body and look through his or her eyes; press Escape again to go back). This is not always the best choice, though. You really do get a better sense of your surroundings if you stay in third person and use the Camera Controls. And, in crowded or laggy areas—like Popular Places—the Camera can move even if your avatar gets stuck.

Using Search: The Land Sales Page

The Land Sales tab page is where land for sale should be listed (see Figure 4.18). However, the usefulness of this page for both buyers and sellers is diminished—believe it or not—because the Classified tab "comes first." That is to say, most people have been conditioned to read tabs from left to right. Also, we tend to click on the first tab that's labeled even vaguely like the thing we want to find. Hence, the land for sale listings in the Classifieds, even though the category name is actually Land (or Property) for Rent.

There are two very important considerations involved in buying land, and price isn't either of them. These potential boondoggles are prims and zoning—information that doesn't always appear in the Classifieds, and rarely comes up in the big list of Search results. So how do you read a Land Sales listing? Set aside the matter of price at first. Gaze at the pretty pictures, choose a location to visit based on looks (just for now), and click the blue Teleport button.

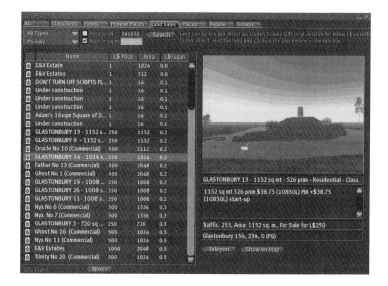

FIGURE 4.18 The Land Sales tab page in the Search dialog box.

The Agony and Ecstasy of Prims

While you can wear and attach an infinite number of prims to your avatar's body, the number of prims you can set down on land is severely restricted. The smallest size lot that's relatively inhabitable—512 sq/m—only gives you 117 prims to work with. That's sounds like a lot, right? It's not: there are probably that many prims in your avatar's hairstyle alone. So it's easy to understand why residents will pay a lot of real-world money for large chunks of virtual land. Quite simply, you have to have a lot of land to be able to build something cool, because you need a lot of land to get a lot of prims. (We will go into prims, land, and building in greater detail later on, in Chapters 6, 7, and 8.)

Some Second Life landlords have designed their rentable land in such a way as to give you more than the minimum number of allowable prims. But generally speaking, you should never assume that you'll get more than the minimum. So how do you calculate that minimum number? Take the size of a piece of land in square meters and plug it into this formula (in this example, we're using 4,096 sq/m):

1. Multiply the land size number (4,096) by 15,000. In this example, you get 61,440,000.

2. Divide this number by 65,536. In this example, you get 937.5 for an answer.

3. This means land that measures 4,096 sq/m should come with a minimum of 937 prims. (Unfortunately, you can't round up and get 938.)

Zoning and Land Use in Second Life

Just like in real life, there are different types of land usage zones in Second Life: residential, commercial, and mixed use. These distinctions will affect your quest for land, regardless of the type you choose for yourself. Why? Sometimes in SL, landlords are not careful about zoning or discriminating about their tenants. So you need to know who your neighbors are, and what they are doing right alongside your land.

Residential land has been specifically restricted, by the owner, for houses and other living space only. Tenants on residential land may still build things for sale on this land, but they can't construct stores or other spaces for doing business. Other residents in residential zones take this restriction very seriously, as businesses draw lots of foot traffic and create lag for everybody.

Commercial land is specifically restricted, often developed, and terraformed by the owner to accommodate business builds only. Tenants and visitors to these spaces expect to encounter increased lag and accept more of it as a matter of course—although wise landlords will work hard to keep lag low, as too much of it will eventually drive customers *and* tenants away.

Mixed zone land may be used for any purpose—residential or commercial or even both. In reality, most mixed zones are occupied by commercial tenants (see the discussion regarding lag previously). But if you do create a store in a mixed zone and you have residential neighbors, they are less likely to complain about lag. They decided to take their chances when they moved in.

There's another thought to keep in mind when considering zones. Remember you have eight neighbors, not four. There might be four lots directly to the north, south, east, and west of the land you're considering. But you should also look at the four lots near the corners. The reason for this has to do with audible privacy. Once you get within 20 meters of anyone else in SL, whether you can see them or not, you will "overhear" them. You will be able to hear the key-clicking sound effects of another resident typing, and you'll be able to see their words in open chat. Also, of course, they will be able to overhear you. So choose land carefully, and if you can afford it, cost should not be your first consideration.

Using Search: The Places and People Pages

The Places and the People tab pages are by far the most often-used parts of Search. However, you have to use distinctly different strategies to come up with optimal results. Let's start with a look at the Places tab page (see Figure 4.19).

The Places page breaks down into 12 distinct categories, not including the Any Category tab. All of them have one thing in common: you can't just browse. The Search button will only "turn on" and become clickable if you type a keyword in the text box first. For all practical purposes, this means you really have to know—already—what you are looking for.

The People tab page, on the other hand, is designed for finding other residents when you can't remember their entire, exact names (see Figure 4.20). You can type in the first name, the last name, or part of either of these names, and get "smart" results. In other words, if you remember meeting somebody who called himself Sam, you can type in "sam" and get all possible first and last names with "sam" in them. Once you find the name of the avatar you are looking for, click it once and that resident's Profile will appear on the right side of the dialog box.

Name amnesia will happen far more often than you think. Second Life has an elegant solution to help you remember: the calling card. Calling cards are incredibly useful as reminders, but most residents don't seem inclined to exchange them. This might be a user interface problem; the Add Card functionality is on the second "page" of the pie menu and therefore not necessarily easy

FIGURE 4.19 The Places tab page in the Search dialog box.

FIGURE 4.20 The People tab page in the Search dialog box.

friend *v.* To add another resident to your Friends list. If the resident is nearby, you can click his or her nameplate and choose Add Friend from the pie menu. If the resident is not around or even offline, click the blue Friends button to open the Friends dialog box, click the Add Friend button, and type in the full, exact name of the avatar to be added.

to grab or remember. So you are very likely to meet someone interesting, and only remember part of his or her name later on unless you "**friend**" each other. (There's a lot more information about calling cards, friendship, and other social considerations in Chapter 5, "Designing Your Social Life," if you want more details.)

Using Search: The Groups Page

So now you know how to find a place, an event, a type of event, a specific business, and even the Profile of a particular resident. But how do you increase the chance of meeting many residents who share your interest in spelunking, or your need to discuss economics? You look for Groups by searching the Groups page (see Figure 4.21).

FIGURE 4.21 The Groups tab page in the Search dialog box. (results for "vampire")

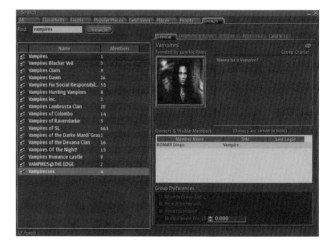

There is a catch or two involved in finding success, and therefore Groups, using this area of Search. First, think broadly. Maybe you're a fan of a specific vampire culture, something written about in a series of novels or explored in a popular game. However, the Groups Search function only matches keywords to Group titles. You'd be better off searching with "vampire" and wading through all the various choices. Or, alternatively, try searching with the proper name of your favorite vampire clan, or its sire or leader.

Also, some Groups might have hundreds of members. (The number to the right of a Group name tells you how many residents currently belong.) This stat might seem akin to traffic numbers, and lead you to believe the Group is active as well as popular. This is not necessarily the case; you need to read the description of the Group and figure out its purpose. Some Groups are only formed to exchange information, or to serve a short-term function. These Groups are less likely to provide the kind of entrée into Second Life society you might be seeking.

After you find a Group that seems interesting, dig down a little and learn what you can from the Search results. The most friendly and welcoming Groups do not charge a fee to join, and they list the names and titles of their members. You will learn the most about a Group as a nonmember by scrolling down the member list and double-clicking the bolded names. These residents are the Group's owners, and therefore the people who created or manage the group. Send one of them a polite, friendly IM asking for more information, even if you can (and do) join the group for free.

Joining a Group will enable you to get even more information. It will subscribe you to the Group chat, so you can listen in on real-time conversations or announcements. Joining also enables you to receive notices—announcement messages that get saved for you and sent as email if you've set up that preference. Group members can also click the blue Detailed View button to read archives of previous notices and see which other Group members are currently online. All this information will enable you to make contact, get involved, and stay involved with other residents who share your interests.

Don't Do It!

If you've discovered the Add Friend feature and the Friends list, you might be thinking it's far easier to just offer friendship to anybody who stops to chat. This might be fine for newer residents, but long-time inhabitants of Second Life are likely to feel otherwise. For one thing, up until fairly recently, "friending" someone meant giving up a certain amount of privacy—this is why there are check boxes at the bottom of the Friends list now, allowing you to decide who can and cannot see or track you. This historical fact still lingers, and can make a quick offer of friendship feel intrusive or badly timed, or just plain rude. Also, you don't want somebody to accept your friendship because they don't want to seem rude by turning you down. So if you really want to be friends, ask first. It never, ever hurts.

ADDITIONAL CREDITS

You can find all the brand, style, color, and designer information on items shown in the figures in the online appendix you get when registering your book at at www.peachpit.com/secondlife. See page v for details.

chapter 5

DESIGNING YOUR SOCIAL LIFE

There's no question that Second Life is fun to explore. There's always something happening and always something new to see. However, SL is first and foremost a community of people—a wonderful place to meet others, hang out, and become friends.

Second Life is also, increasingly, a mechanism for real-world communication and commerce. This means that you can use SL not just to make social connections, but also to make money. Jobs or careers in SL are yet another way to explore your interests, and to meet other residents who are interested in what you like.

You're also probably going to want to get involved in one or more of the various "subcultures" in Second Life. But there's a difference between just putting on the right clothes and actually finding your niche. This chapter attempts to take some of the "wannabe" out of making personal connections in Second Life, so you can (hopefully) find acquaintances, friends, and even virtual romance a little more easily.

Social Etiquette in Second Life

Whenever two people interact, there's etiquette involved. It might not be the bow-and-curtsy, meet-the-Queen kind of thing (Second Life is, for the most part, quite relaxed and casual). But there are certain specific ways you can be annoying, and boundaries you really should not cross, that might not occur to you. If you're new to SL, you might not know the subtle cultural stuff. If you're still bewildered by the notion that virtual manners actually matter, that's (obviously) going to be an obstacle, too. So before we talk about *shoulds* and *shouldn'ts*, let's take a brief moment to discuss these matters in the abstract.

Why Bother Being Nice? (A Little Game Theory)

Thus far in the book, we've been restating the same idea over and over: Second Life is not a game. However—SL has the appearance of a game, and (here's the theory part) Linden Lab did have games in mind when they created it. Linden Lab wanted to create an environment that provided more features, more freedom, and more flexibility than the average desktop or console game. There's no question that they succeeded in that regard. But Linden Lab also had to understand more than a little game theory in order to produce a "non-game." You have to know how something works before you can improve it.

The goal that all game developers try to reach is both simple and complex: they strive to get a player emotionally involved. If a game bores you, if it's too difficult or too easy, or if you don't care where the storyline is headed, then you'll walk away. A well-designed game, on the other hand, breaks down any sense of separation between the player and the hero. The player starts to want what the hero wants, so he or she is willing to stick around.

Linden Lab went all out to achieve this goal. There's nothing artificially imposed on Second Life residents—no storyline with the usual obstacles, challenges, setbacks, or Big Reveals. Linden Lab handed all the best goodies in games to every resident on a big silver platter, and Second Life residents have gobbled them up. The result is a twist on the player-hero connection described just above. In SL, there's even less emotional and psychological distance than ever between a resident and the person behind the resident. Many SL residents feel personally invested in the future of SL as a medium, a community, and a grand experiment.

Why Do We Even Care?

IF YOU'VE EVER BEEN in a virtual world within range of somebody being violent or disturbing the peace, you probably got irritated. Maybe your annoyance was mild, or maybe you really got upset. In either case, maybe you also wondered why that other person's behavior even got under your skin in the first place. If the situation were real, we reason, then a strong reaction would make sense. So why can't people sometimes separate their reactions between the real and the virtual?

Quite literally, we can't: our brain doesn't make the distinction. It turns out that certain neurons—called mirror neurons—will fire exactly the same way both when we perform an action *and* when we see another person perform it, too. These same neurons are also "interested," as researchers put it, both when we feel an emotional reaction, and when we see someone else's face as they have the same reaction. This is why football fans get into such a frenzy when their team leaps off the bench to celebrate, why actors in agony on film make moviegoers cry—and, why irritating person-shaped avatars succeed in making other residents feel genuinely, thoroughly, irritated. People just can't help it. We're hardwired this way.

Ergo, in-world emotions stir genuine responses. If you don't pay your virtual rent, or don't keep your virtual promises, you're going to provoke a real problem. SL is not a game in any way, and neither are the feelings of those who populate it.

What does all this have to do with manners and etiquette? For starters, there's no refuge for those who act aggressively or childishly in Second Life because the "protective barrier" of a storyline does not exist. In other online worlds where (for example) there's an ongoing war, there's a modest amount of tolerance for the player who walks up to strangers and bashes them with weapons. Is this rude and frowned on and unwelcome? Of course. But there's ambiance and tension to be maintained. So even on a subconscious level, every player in that world knows unsociable behavior needs to be tolerated unless it gets markedly out of hand.

In Second Life, there's no such architecture—Linden Lab just provides the raw materials. Residents built (and are building) the SL world, and drive the economy, and decide what's permitted where. Residents even create the storyline, if there's any storyline at all. Residents, therefore, are much more deeply invested in SL than in any online game. So if you make residents irritated; if you ignore what other residents prefer and expect; if you can't (or won't) control your baser impulses, then you'll be persona non grata in no time flat. As a result, because SL is ultimately a means of communication, your bad behavior could limit your abilities to expand your horizons.

The Big Six Revisited: More on Second Life Community Standards

In Chapter 1, we covered The Big Six community standards that Linden Lab upholds. These six no-nos are: Intolerance, Harassment, Assault, Disclosure, Indecency, and Disturbing the Peace. In the real world, these offenses are fairly well defined, and the majority of people know when they are taking place. But in the metaverse, there are SL-specific ways to break these laws. So let's revisit the Big Six and expand on their meanings just a little more.

Intolerance

Intolerance—Acting or speaking in such a way that "marginalizes, belittles, or defames" somebody based on his or her gender, sexual orientation, race, ethnicity, or religion.

Intolerance also, sometimes, involves the type of shape or in-world activity a resident chooses to embrace. Some residents will gives other residents a hard time for walking around in a semi- or non-human shape, or for using Second Life to role-play by very specific, even strict rules. Intolerance of this nature doesn't just upset the victims; it often annoys uninvolved bystanders, too. So don't do it, and don't put up with it. Others surely won't.

Harassment

Harassment—Anything said or done that makes someone else feel alarmed, upset, intimidated, or uncomfortable.

The scenario that leaps to most people's minds when they hear the word "harassment" involves one person who's scantily clad and another person who's responding inappropriately. Second Life Harassment also involves using in-world tools and features to bug another resident. Persistent IMs, invitations to teleport, and offered Inventory items, or returning or deleting another's objects, are all prime examples of Harassment. So if somebody says no, to anything, that "no" should be respected.

Assault

Assault—Pushing, shoving, shooting, attacking someone using something scripted, or otherwise making somebody unsafe in a Safe area.

Yes, it's true that in most areas, the "safety is on" and in-world weapons, spells, and other life-threatening stuff will not actually kill another avatar. Yes, it's also true that a resident has to be wearing a health meter in an Unsafe area to actually be hurt or killed. But you don't have to be risking another resident's virtual life and safety to be violating this rule. If, for example, you shoot at another resident and make him feel he has to avoid your bullets, you're committing Assault. If you use a script to send a resident into orbit and she didn't agree to it first, you're committing Assault. In short, if your actions cause another resident to move when they weren't intending to move, you're committing Assault. Don't do it.

Disclosure

Disclosure—Any action that reveals an aspect of somebody's real-life identity that they have not shared publicly in their Profile.

This should also be a no-brainer in the virtual world, because anybody with a computer and an Internet connection knows identity protection is a serious concern. So it shouldn't be surprising that this violation is considered the worst of the Big Six, by residents of Second Life and probably by Linden Lab as well. Therefore, do not ever compromise a resident's privacy, even if he or she has given *you* that personal information. It doesn't matter if what you know won't give away a name, location, or other unique identifier. Residents of Second Life have the right to decide for themselves how much, or how little, of their real selves they want to share.

Indecency

Indecency—Doing something M in a PG area, or in front of another resident who is bothered by your actions.

In some cases, Indecency is pretty obvious: the guy running around wearing nothing but enormous naughty bits, for example. In others, honestly, it's a matter of personal opinion. If you're in a store with your SL sweetie, teasing each other in a raunchy fashion, that can be considered Indecent by certain residents. If you "overhear" someone getting it on because you wander into chat range, even if you can't see him, you could argue that he is being Indecent. So, in summary, Indecency is about any behavior that can be construed as sexual or sensual, occurring in the wrong place. Use your common sense and you won't ever be accused of this particular faux pas.

Disturbing the Peace

Disturbing the Peace—If you do, say, build, or put something on the ground that makes a racket, you're disturbing the peace.

Everybody in Second Life has the right to quiet if he wants it, but here's the twist: there are two types of "noise" in SL. There's the kind that reaches your ears—muscle cars have big engines and gardens are filled with twittery birds. There's also the kind of "noise," however, that fills up your eyes. Visual noise, for lack of a better way to describe it, is caused by objects that "talk" and use up the chat window buffer. If you're nearby these sorts of things, you literally cannot get a word in edgewise—but casinos and certain kinds of stores, and other popular types of destinations, can't do without them. So this particular violation of the service agreement can be stridently debated if you disturb someone's peace. Is that how you really want to spend your time in-world? Didn't think so.

Breaking the Ice:
Meeting, Greeting, and Just Hanging Out

Real-world conversation is a symphony of words, facial expressions, tone of voice, and body language. In-world conversation is, by contrast, pretty flat. Even if you add animations or gestures to the mix, you're relying mostly on words. **Animations** and **gestures** are widely used in Second Life, but you don't necessarily see them in action if they are used correctly. This is why it pays to invest some time and money outfitting your avatar with good ones. You want to make other residents feel comfortably at ease when you're around, even if they don't necessarily register the reason why in a conscious way.

Speaking Without Words: Animations and Gestures

Residents rely on anims and gestures to make their avatars look as natural as possible. Linden Lab provides a certain degree of twitchiness, for example, your avatar will breathe, blink erratically and turn his or her head toward whomever is "speaking." But the default way your avatar will stand or sit looks anything but realistic. For one thing, these defaults are designed to be somewhat unisex, although they make female avatars look somewhat masculine (see Figure 5.1).

ꭍLanguage

animation *n.* A set of scripted instructions that gives any object motion, including an avatar. Also called an "anim" for short. May loop continuously until deactivated or only occur once.

gesture *n.* A combination of synchronized animations and sounds. A gesture may be linked to a trigger or a specific word, so that "saying" the word in open chat activates the gesture. A gesture may also be initiated with shortcut keys.

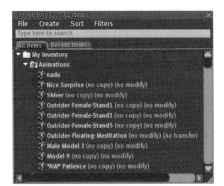

FIGURE 5.2 Animations in the Inventory dialog box.

FIGURE 5.1 The default just-hanging-around poses: stiff, hyper-alert, and uncomfortable.

FIGURE 5.3 The Animation dialog box.

To find an animation, click the blue Inventory button near the lower-right corner of the Second Life window. The Inventory dialog box will open; scroll down to the Animations folder and open it (see Figure 5.2).

To preview an animation, double-click the animation icon in the Inventory dialog box, and the Animation dialog box will open (see Figure 5.3). You'll have two choices: Play in World and Play Locally. The Play Locally option allows you to preview an animation; your avatar will move but nobody else will see it. The Play in World option, by contrast, allows everybody to see the animation after you've decided it's the one you want. However, that's not the most efficient or common way to use animations in Second Life.

Animations are designed to be dropped into objects called **AO**s, or animation overrides, which run the anims automatically. An AO allows you to substitute animations of your choice for Second Life's defaults, such as standing, sitting, running, and walking. For the purposes of making your avatar seem more life-like, there are two types of AOs—premade ones with a selection of animations already installed, or blank ones you can "program" after you buy the individual animations you like best. Preprogrammed AOs are easier to use; you just buy and wear them. Programmable AOs are available for free, but the animations

♪Language

AO *n.* Short for "animation override." An animation override is a scripted object that replaces Second Life's default animations with resident-created animations. You can purchase a prebuilt AO already loaded up with replacement anims, or get a blank AO for free and fill it with your own choices.

themselves are not. So the cost can easily equal out after you add up the total price. A good AO is certainly worth the investment, so it is advisable to get one fairly early on, whether you want to customize it or not.

One of the best features of an AO is how you use it. You wear an AO as an attachment, either somewhere inconspicuous on your avatar's body or as a **HUD**. HUDs are a fantastic way to keep all your essential controls within easy reach, without blocking your view with a menu or dialog box, or taking up an attachment slot on your avatar's body. You don't necessarily have to choose between HUDs, either, as there are eight slots for HUDs at different stations all along the Second Life window. Some HUDs are even completely invisible, so you can situate them somewhere on the SL window where you would ordinarily be annoyed to see tools or controls. The end result is well worth the tweaking, too. Figure 5.4 shows a number of example AO-controlled animations that look far more natural and easy on the eyes than the defaults in Figure 5.1.

Profiles Revisited: Finding Commonalities

Fortunately, most Second Life residents will respond if you're friendly and polite. But SL can still sometimes feel like one big cocktail party when you're fresh out of small talk. So how can you figure out which residents might have things in common with you, if chitchat feels awkward? Here's a strategy for sifting through profiles: Bartle's Quotient.

If you think Bartle's Quotient sounds like the results from some sort of personality quiz, you're not too far off the mark. Richard Bartle is a founding father of the gaming industry; he wrote a famous series of questions designed to measure the interests and preferences of online gamers. Bartle groups gamers into four distinct categories: achievers, explorers, socializers, and killers. Achievers seek the prestige and the bling; explorers want to find every last secret, nook, and cranny; socializers need to interact with other people; killers crave conflict in any form they can find it. Everybody in a virtual world wants all of these things to a greater or lesser degree. But one category tends to dominate each player's psychology percentage-wise, and that's the information that makes up Bartle's Quotient.

This isn't just a theoretical observation. The Wikipedia entry on Bartle's Test says that as of January 2007, over a quarter of a million people have taken the test to see how they score. Also, game developers have used Bartle's categories for years to try to gauge why games work or fail, and what consumers want. Typically, a game will succeed in serving the needs of one or two groups but not

ʃLanguage

HUD *n.* Short for "heads-up display." A type of scripted object that attaches somewhere along the edge of the Second Life window. HUDs enable you to see or access controls much more quickly than if you had to open a menu or dialog box. Most HUDs will therefore be items you'll use all the time, such as AOs, regardless of whatever you're wearing or doing.

FIGURE 5.4 Slightly more natural-looking "standing" animations.

Animations Plus: Second Life Gestures

If you've ever made a macro in Microsoft Word, or even a presentation in Microsoft PowerPoint, then you already get the general idea of a gesture. A gesture in Second Life is a sequence of actions, sounds, words, and pauses your avatar will act out in the precise order you specify. A gesture makes use of animations, but it also includes sound files, bits of "dialogue" that appears in the chat textbox, and "waits" to make any transitions between animations look natural. Most of the time, gestures are used for emphasis or just to goof around and be funny. But occasionally, a custom gesture is the icing on the cake, especially if you get into a situation (like an in-world meeting) where you are making a presentation or otherwise leading a discussion. See the Second Life Knowledge Base for more detailed information on how to make use of this feature.

the others. Second Life, however, is arguably the first online environment to satisfy all four groups because residents have created all the content.

What does all this have to do with meeting people in Second Life? A lot. Chances are pretty good that your Quotient shines through on your Profile. Residents don't use or refer to the Quotient in a conscious manner. ("Hey, baby, what's your Quotient?" won't get you anywhere.) But if you're looking for other residents who might have interests in common with yours, the idea of Quotient may help you out when you're looking at Profiles.

Here are some Profile-related clues that might give you insight into another resident's Quotient:

- **Achievers**—Highest-quality portraits; membership in multiple VIP Groups; Picks relating to the most popular places, the stores of the hottest, most noteworthy designers, or ways to measure what's trendy

- **Explorers**—Portraits seemingly taken on the fly in someplace beautiful; not many Group memberships; lots of Picks dedicated to destinations that offer highly creative builds or tantalizing/unusual things to do

- **Socializers**—High-quality portraits focused on the face; lots of Group memberships, with or without rhyme or reason; many Picks paying tribute to friends, "family," or other social affiliations

- **Killers**—Portraits taken "in character" in some sort of period or RP outfit, perhaps with weapons displayed; membership in Groups that sound battle-, strategy-, or territory-oriented; Picks that advertise loyalty, fealty, or affiliations to such aforementioned Groups

Another tip is to pay attention to the title a resident is wearing over his or her name. The title, remember, displays a resident's membership in a Group; it also gives brief clues to the role that resident plays within that Group. So it's easy, and sometimes necessary, to switch from title to title, depending on where you are and what you're doing. To select a title to wear, right- or Apple-click on your avatar to open the Pie menu and choose Groups. The Groups dialog box will appear (see Figure 5.5).

To select a title to wear, click once on the Group of your choice and click the blue Activate button. The Group you chose will be bolded, letting you know it's been selected, so click Close. You should see your chosen Group title just above your avatar's name.

One last tip about titles and Groups. Many residents leave on their favorite titler, or the one that means the most to them personally. In some ways, this is like allowing other residents to read a bit of your mind. So if you see a title over a resident's head that hints at something you find interesting, an excellent way to initiate conversation is to ask about it politely. Chances are pretty good that the resident is glad to talk about whatever group, friends, or preferred pastimes that their title represents (see Figure 5.6).

FIGURE 5.5 The Groups' dialog box.

FIGURE 5.6 Interesting titlers, interesting Groups, social opportunities.

Making Connections: Calling Cards and Friends

Once you've met another resident and hit it off, there are two ways to keep the connection going. The first way is not used as often as it should be: calling cards. The second way is somewhat abused and not well understood: friendship. Let's cover the merits and drawbacks, and appropriate use, of both.

A *calling card* is a type of shortcut with your name on it (see Figure 5.7). It's stored in the Inventory like an object, and opens your Profile if someone double-clicks it. When you have someone's calling card (and they have yours), you can use the card in your Inventory to start an IM, invite the resident to a conference chat, send a TP, or open that resident's Profile.

All of these options are in the calling card submenu (see Figure 5.8). To open that submenu, click the blue Inventory button in the lower-right corner of the Second Life window to open your Inventory. Scroll down to find the Calling Cards folder. Click once on the triangle to the left to open the folder, find the calling card you want, and right- or Apple-click on it to reveal the submenu.

FIGURE 5.7 Calling cards in your Inventory.

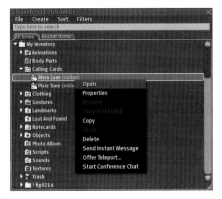

FIGURE 5.8 The Calling Card submenu.

To give someone your calling card, click on that resident to open the Pie menu and then choose More > Give Card. Both of you will see a blue message window appear in the lower-right corner of the Second Life screen stating that the card was offered. A card may be accepted or declined; in either case, you'll see another blue message window telling you what happened.

So, in summary, you can do all the things with a calling card that many over-eager residents use friendship offers to do. So why do so many residents jump the gun? Offering friendship instead of a calling card, especially to near-strangers, is rude. In fact, it's one of the most unintentionally annoying things

FIGURE 5.9 The Friends list dialog box.

one resident can do to another, although newcomers wouldn't know that. In all fairness, this disconnect (and total irony) probably has to do with a few social and technical considerations:

○ Offering friendship might seem like the thing to do in order to be perceived as kind, grateful, approachable, etc., in return to someone who has been all those things to you.

○ The Friends list is prominently displayed and very easy to access (there's no equivalent list for calling cards).

○ It takes effort to remember that Add Card is on the Pie menu *and* one level down from the top menu "layer," that is, not at all an obvious feature.

○ The potential problems involved in friending another resident too quickly aren't obvious, either, so newcomers don't realize what they are asking for.

So what is friendship in Second Life, above and beyond adding a resident's name to your Friends list? Let's begin by taking a closer look at the Friends list (see Figure 5.9).

Friending someone can set up a certain expectation between two residents, because there are other significant advantages/features that only friends can see or do. Take another look at Figure 5.9 and focus on the check boxes near the bottom of the dialog box. These options correspond to the icons along the top of the list. The presence or absence of these icons next to a friend's name represents certain special types of permissions.

To give a friend permissions, click once on his or her name in the Friends list dialog box. You'll notice that this makes two of the three check boxes at the bottom of the box turn "on" and become clickable. You can give a friend the ability to see whether you are online or not, and to see when you enter or leave Second Life.

Check the first check box about online status if you want to give a friend this option, and two things will happen. One, a little blue eye will appear in the first column to the right of the selected friend's name. Two, the second check box option will turn on; if you check this box, a little blue square will appear next to the selected friend's name as well. Now this friend will be able to see you coming and going, and be able to use the Map to **track** you.

To track a friend, click the blue Map button near the lower-right corner of the Second Life window. The Map dialog box will open (see Figure 5.10). There's

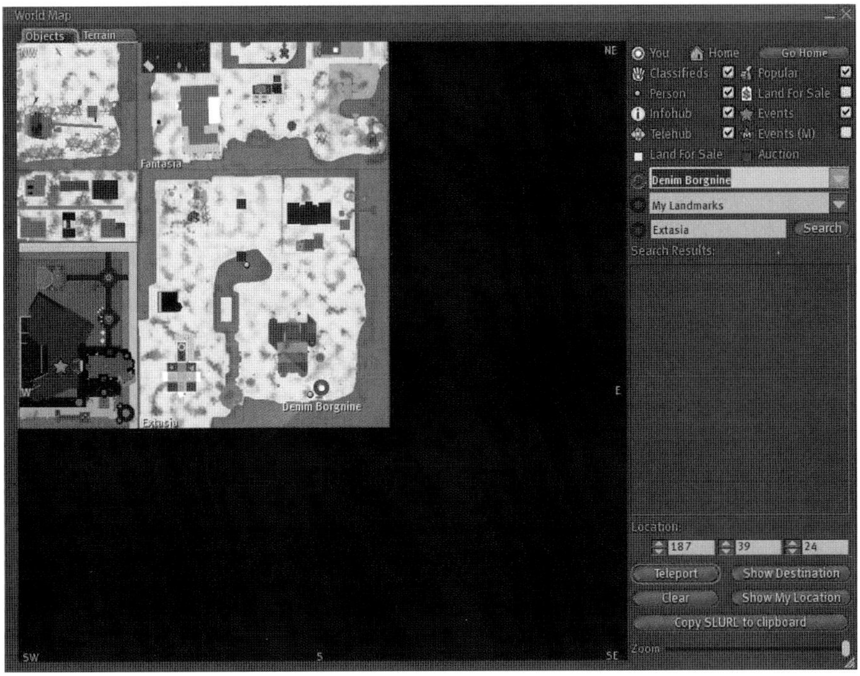

FIGURE 5.10 The Map dialog box: tracking a friend.

a drop-down menu near the upper-right corner labeled "My Friends." If you have friends that allow you to see their online status and their location on the grid, you can type in their names or choose them from this menu. The Map will zoom to where they are, and allow you to click Teleport and pop up at their side. This is why it's crucial to ask permission first *before* tracking. If anything naughty or otherwise Mature is going on, you don't want to suddenly appear at an awkward moment. (That's the fastest way to end a friendship.)

The other two icons near the top-right corner of the Friends list dialog box have to do with modifying objects. As you can see, there's one last checkable option at the bottom of this same dialog box: Can Modify My Objects. If you click on a friend's name to select it and then check this box, you have given your friend the ability to edit or delete anything you've built. A small icon that looks like a hand passing over a cube will then appear next to your friend's name. If there's another similar icon next to your friends' names here, then they have given you the capability to edit/delete their things.

This brings us back to friendship and expectations. Most residents of Second Life know better than to expect permissions from friends; most won't ever ask for them, either. But there's always going to be some yahoo who'll get offended because he expects them as your friend. Furthermore, there are always going to be people who expect you to reciprocate if they give you permissions. In both situations, you might be very glad you didn't give such people any perks, because friends-with-perks who get mad at you can wreak all kinds of havoc.

So to a certain extent, you should treat friendship in SL as if all these buttons and menus are mislabeled. Calling cards are all you need for being friends in the actual sense of the word—for keeping in touch, for sending messages, for sending TPs. "Friendship," as Second Life defines it, should be reserved for those you really know and really trust.

Hookups, Dating, and Partnerships in Second Life

If you meet someone who really rocks your virtual world, you might want to go farther than just being friends. There are plenty of dark corners in Second Life with naughty poseballs for a quick hookup. There are also many places that are perfect for a nice, romantic, get-to-know-you-better kind of date. There are also many merchants and designers making a good virtual living as wedding planners. Yes, in Second Life (as in many other online worlds or games) you can "marry" your extra special online friend. Linden Lab even allows you to make it "official," with the Partner feature.

Those are the facts. In practice, of course, hookups, dating, and even partnerships are largely social activities. To wit, there's no technical benefit to making any of these distinctions, not as there are potentially between friends. But this practical fact doesn't stop residents from singling out other residents and giving them a special place in their online lives.

Pairing Up in Second Life

So how do you go about making a match in Second Life? Just like you go about it in real life, more or less. Look for compatibilities, then look for roadblocks, and finally proceed if the other person gives you the enthusiastic, encouraging green light. We've already talked about how to make educated guesses regarding other residents and if you both have things in common. So let's dwell on the middle part of that "plan" for a while: potential obstacles to romance.

General Design Advice: Real-World Communication

There are many Second Life residents who do communicate with each other outside the SL world. But they do so in such a way that usually protects their real-life identities. So if you are designing your Second Life to allow for crossover, consider signing up for one or more of the following free methods of online communication:

- Some sort of free email account, with a service such as Yahoo, MSN, Hotmail, or Gmail (if another Gmail user will send you an invite).
- Some sort of free chat account, with a service such as Microsoft Messenger, Yahoo Chat, or ICQ.
- A Skype or Google Talk account so you can talk "on the phone" for free if you have, or can afford, headphones and a mike.

You can make a relatively seamless transition between Second Life and these real-life communication options if you use your avatar's name to establish all these accounts. This is also a good strategy for protecting your anonymity, although you should spend a little time cleaning out the profiles these services create for you. However, with a little effort, these communication options can enhance your Second Life if you are comfortable using them that way.

No matter what your reason for wanting to get to know another resident better, romantically speaking, here are a few signs to look for:

○ If you browse a resident's Picks, and you see a romantic or sexual portrait topping off some mushy tribute —especially if there's a specific date somewhere in all that text—that's an S.O. type relationship.

○ If you see a big flash on a female resident's left hand, or a band on a male avatar's left hand, those are wedding rings all right. That kind of jewelry, in that place on the body, means the same thing in SL as it does in the real world: that resident is spoken for.

○ If you see anything around a resident's neck that looks like a collar—a single band sitting high on the throat, usually with a loop on the front—that's also the equivalent of commitment jewelry in some social circles.

○ If you see a set of bands around an avatar's wrists, ankles, or upper arms that are all the same color (especially if that avatar is also wearing a collar), this is also a sign that girl or guy is "taken."

○ If you're on a role-playing SIM where the storyline is specific to certain time periods in western European or American history, look at women's hair. Sometimes unmarried girls wore their hair loose because married women were required to wear it up. Or married women wore frilly white caps because only single women could wear their hair uncovered.

○ If you see a name in the Partner text box, located near the upper-right corner of the 2nd Life tab page on a resident's Profile, this is the most obvious "I'm-taken" type of sign.

Sometimes, a resident's objection to getting romantic has nothing to do with his or her Second Life at all. Sometimes that resident's real-life romantic situation means no online romance. Or maybe that person just isn't interested in online coupling. It's his or her call. The point is this: If someone tells you no-thanks, don't push or pry or challenge it. Just back off.

This also needs to be said: an in-world romantic connection does not imply or guarantee a real-life connection. It doesn't give you the right to know anything about a resident's real life, not even a name or a real-life time zone location. If you make any sort of effort to set one resident apart from all your other friends, then you should never, ever expect the object of your affection to be something more. This doesn't mean you should assume someone is married with kids, trying to "play around on the side" and hide it. It simply means that every SL resident is entitled to any degree of privacy that he or she wants.

Adding a Partner to Your Second Life

Partnership in Second Life is quite similar to other SL features—it is, or isn't, what you make of it. If your reasons for wanting partnership are romantic, you have to go out and find the ring, collar, or other traditional symbol of choice (depends on the tradition, remember). You can get yourself an animation or poseball that allows you get down on one knee. You can also choose to spend a not-so-small fortune on the wedding of your dreams, complete with cathedral, reception, and even a posh tropical honeymoon (see Figure 5.11).

From a technical standpoint, the requirements for partnership are considerably less fairy-tale. If you want to propose partnership, go to the Second Life Web site and click the Community link. If you scroll down the page, glance through the menu options in blue along the left side until you see the section called My Second Life. The last choice in this subsection is Partners. Click that link, and the Partnership Proposal page will appear.

Enter your name, compose your proposal text, and send it off. Your S.O.-to-be will receive word of your proposal in two ways. The proposal will be sent as email to the email address he or she gave during account setup, and it's also visible if he or she logs in and goes to the Partnership Proposal page. There is a

FIGURE 5.11 Mazeltov! Congratulations! (A good excuse to buy some really nice clothes.)

FIGURE 5.12 Partnership accomplished: your newly updated Profile.

small fee that each partner has to pay in order for Linden Lab to change your Profiles. But if your bride or groom clicks *I Do*, you'll be partnered. The SL Web site tells you so, and you'll see the change in your Profiles, too (see Figure 5.12).

If the partnership goes south, the partner seeking divorce will have to pay another small fee for the uncoupling. To revoke (i.e., break up) a partnership, go back to the Partners page on the Second Life Web site. All you have to do is check the box provided, click Submit, and that's that.

Pregnancy and Children in Second Life

Another popular carryover from real life, believe it or not, is having children. That's right: a positive pregnancy test, getting big around the middle, going to the doctor, the whole shebang. From a technical perspective, Second Life childbearing is a combination of wearing different shapes; role-playing interaction; special poseballs; and a baby-shaped armful of prims. Socially speaking, it's a group experience among you, your sweetie, the staff of whatever clinic you choose, and (later on, if you want) another resident who takes on the role of playing your child.

A quick, informal survey of the most popular childbirth clinics revealed a fairly standard M.O. The mother-to-be (or the couple) purchases a birth package for a lump sum. Birth packages typically contain a series of progressively pregnant body shapes, a variety of medical exams and appointments including the birth, and sometimes also a custom-made infant (or two if you go for twins). Other extras may include spa appointments for mom; custom layettes; animations or poses for interacting with the infant; baby pictures; or discounts with maternity wear designers.

The length of a pregnancy is entirely customizable, too. Another entirely unscientific survey discovered that "typical" couples decide to be pregnant for anywhere from 27 days (3 days per "month") or 9 weeks (1 week per "month"). It depends on how much fun the couple wants to have as parents-to-be—to buy stuff for the nursery or build a bigger house to have a nursery, if friends are throwing baby showers, and so on (see Figure 5.13).

FIGURE 5.13 Second Life childbearing: from special body shapes to actual infants and the animations to hold them, it's as real as you make it.

What's not "typical" in this scenario? Pregnancies that occur within a larger role-playing framework, to residents also RPing a goth, Gorean, Victorian, paranormal, Wild West, furry, or other sort of storyline, too. If the parents-to-be want to stay as authentic as possible to the rules of their "world," the duration of the pregnancy can change, or the number of babies, or maybe there needs to be a shotgun wedding. Again, it's all about the fun, and everybody's type of fun in Second Life is different.

No matter what type of offspring you have, or how you have them, there can be life after babyhood for your children. While Second Life is closed to real-life minors (players under the age of legal consent), there are many SL residents who play children. If you take a good thorough look through Search for adoption agencies, you will find organizations that will match residents who want to continue to be parents and residents who are willing to role-play being children. You can also Search the Classifieds for "loving parents seeking to adopt" or "adoptive children seeking a good home." Of course, this kind of RP would not be practical or convincing if there weren't pint-sized shapes, clothes, etc. Fortunately for residents who are interested, there are designers providing all sorts of stuff in child sizes (see Figure 5.14).

A common, additional option is for residents with infants to team up with other such "parents," and agree to RP older children for each other. This strategy does have certain benefits, in that you know the other resident(s) RPing with you are sincerely interested in that sort of storyline. It also means that you all have the same incentive, so you're all more likely to give what you want to get in return. The best way to meet other such like-minded residents is to use the same strategies as adoption agencies. Advertise in Search, submit Classifieds, and also leave word with the family practice clinic who delivered/provided your infant if you used such a service.

FIGURE 5.14 Children, Continued: what happens when prim babies grow up (sometimes).

Little(r) Avatars in a Mature World

At this writing, there's a lot of discussion going on about children in Second Life—not just the possible presence of actual kids logging on to play adults, which is absolutely verboten. But, also, Lindens and residents alike are debating the merits of child-shaped avatars in any area of SL. Hopefully, it goes without saying that violent or sexual activity including child-shaped avatars is *not* allowed. It should also be obvious that allowing child-shaped avatars to run around in a Mature-rated area is a spectacularly bad idea.

So if you're determined to have an SL family including any "children," be very, very careful. You might think it's the most wholesome, innocent thing in the virtual world to have the spouse-and-kids type of Second Life. But underage-looking avatars simply freak some people out, and your presence alongside that "child" will evoke the same reaction.

Here are some common sense guidelines. Build your family's home on a PG-rated, entirely residential SIM. Don't entrust the roles of your SL children to strangers; if those people turn out to be under 18, you're in a universe of trouble. Keep a close eye on the SL blogs and other places where the rules are posted and updated. Most importantly, if your "kids'" presence is causing a stir, send them away immediately and leave the area yourself. Don't get defensive, don't get offended, just go.

Jobs and Careers in Second Life

For a while now, there's been steady media coverage about residents making real money in Second Life. In one sense, it's true: there are real people who are using SL as a means to earn income. The fine print to this big news is that the amount of money varies greatly. Only a handful of residents hit upon the right idea at the right time and ended up making a living. Most SL residents with in-world jobs or careers are making pocket change, either by SL or real-life standards, depending on how you look at their profits.

Second Life occupations break down roughly into four categories:

○ **Making a Quick Buck**—In-world activities that make enough Lindens for you to go shopping once or twice a month.

○ **Part-Time Work**—Usually service- or retail-type jobs working for another resident in-world, for a handful of hours at wages paid in Lindens.

○ **Free Enterprise**—Working for yourself doing something strictly in-world, by designing, marketing, and selling things you made using SL's tools.

○ **Big Business**—Crossover project development involving real-world businesses, scripting, funding, or any other activity that pays a real-world wage in real-world currency.

Let's discuss each of these options one at a time.

Making a Quick Buck

The majority of Second Life residents really don't need a lot of money to have fun in SL. Many don't even need to pay for their SL accounts because they have little or no desire to own land. So how can you make a little spending money without buying Lindens? There are several options that require very little effort.

Camping is a very popular way to fill your virtual wallet. Residents who "camp" use a specific animated object to keep their avatar in motion for a long period of time. This object can be just a chair with a sitting pose in it. But it can also be a dance pad, a window-washing rig, or a guitar with the case open on the ground, a la street musicians. All these objects deposit Lindens in your avatar's pocket at certain time intervals as long as you leave your avie in place. Expert (or compulsive) campers leave their avatars going all night long.

Why do store- and landowners set out camping anims? To boost traffic stats, which bump their listings higher up the Search results list, and bring more customers by. Remember that traffic in Second Life is not the number of individual avatars that cross the threshold. It's the number of five-minute intervals any avatar spends in one location. So if a mall owner sets out four camping items, and they all get used for eight hours straight, four campers can add almost 390 points to a mall's traffic stats in just one night.

Polling is also a common pastime for business owners and cash-strapped residents to get what they need from each other. This type of activity includes taking surveys; participating in focus groups; walking through partially or fully finished builds to give your opinion; and other marketing-type scenarios. The financial rewards are less predictable than what you can earn with camping, and you have to be conscious at the keyboard to make your money.

Part-Time Work and Free Enterprise

Most jobs in Second Life fall into these two categories, what we call part-time work and free enterprise. Part-time work is just what it sounds like: a handful of hours every real-life week, working for another resident, for an hourly wage. Part-timers are the store clerks, the in-store models, gaming hall attendants, residential estate managers, pole dancers, and all the other employees you see scattered throughout commercial places. Even escorts in bars and clubs (yes, *that* sort of escort) are working for tips and a percentage of fees charged for their services.

Free-enterprisers are on the other side of the desk—the store and SIM owners, the clothing designers, the builders and scripters, the landowners, the weapons makers—entrepreneurs who have a service, product, or experience to sell within Second Life. These residents often employ other residents to do part-time work. But they don't necessarily make lots more money than their employees when all the math is done. Free-enterprisers could be considered SL's middle class, because they are upwardly mobile and highly ambitious. They generally make enough Lindens every 30 days to pay their tier fees. But these residents probably dream of doing far better than breaking even. They dream of turning their SL passion into Big Business.

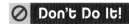

Don't Do It!

All over Second Life, there are scripted objects that will entice you to pay them a few Lindens on the off-chance you might get a whole pile back. Some are obviously gambling or betting machines. But others are labeled as "lucky" or with otherwise half-truth-type descriptions, which could mislead you into paying lots of Lindens. Therefore, here's the deal: it's just as tough in SL to make a living as a professional gambler. So don't get suckered in.

Big Business

When you think Big Business, you might tend to think of companies or corporate entities in the real world like IBM, Nissan, and Wells Fargo (all of whom have or have had a presence in Second Life, by the way). But SL Big Business also includes residents who have parlayed their in-world knowledge and skill into "real" money. These real people have joined forces with Web design agencies, software companies, and other businesses, so their partners can offer SL development as another client service.

There's also the likes of Anshe Chung—perhaps the most savvy Second Life resident, who saw a purely virtual way of making a living and seized it with both hands. These Big Business tycoons are self-employed and flying solo, those who are receiving rather than seeking partnership offers. This is more than likely the scenario that most SL residents hope for: to work for themselves doing something virtual they like best.

Job Listings and Want Ads

There are a couple places, in-world and outside of Second Life, where you can find ads written by residents who are looking for employees—not just part-timers, either, but consultants and per-project work. The first place to look is Search; do keyword searches for the type of job you're looking for ("DJ" and "deejay," just as an example) and also browse the specific sections of the Search listings having to do with employment.

You should also search the Second Life forums at the secondlife.com Web site. These job listings tend to be more in-depth and otherwise detailed about what the job/project/opportunity entails, because the limits on post length aren't as severe as they are in-world. Be aware, though, that job postings in the Forums are actually discussion threads, so be sure to scroll down through the entire thread to look for any additional details. Applicants can post (and not frowned on for posting) questions about hours, salary, and other expectations. So you might find some of your own initial questions answered right there.

Finally, keep an eye open when you're out and about doing any sort of shopping. Many stores will announce job openings on posters or sandwich boards right there on the premises, because proprietors know that fans of their products or services will be the most enthusiastic employees. The only caveat to this type of job search is to follow any instructions spelled out in such ads. Don't IM the owner of the store, in other words, if the ad tells you to speak to a clerk or store manager instead, or you'll make a bad impression.

Exploring Second Life "Subculture"

Most of the social stuff we've covered thus far in this chapter can apply to every resident of Second Life. In fact, you could use everything you've learned and go about your virtual social life fairly well prepared. Indeed, many residents of SL enjoy a "Dick and Jane Avatar" sort of existence in SL that's not necessarily all that different from their real lives (aside from amazing houses, luxury possessions, maintenance-free physiques, and fantastic clothes).

However, there's another segment of the Second Life population, made up of residents whose virtual lives are very different than their real ones. Some want to suspend reality as much as possible, to be the hero in a grand adventure. Others are seeking community and tolerance with those who are into the same alternative lifestyles as they are. The goal for all these residents is to use Second Life to enrich or augment their first lives—to express a part of themselves that doesn't get to come out and play in the real world. For whatever reason, residents who make up these "subcultures" are not unusual or alone. So even if you're not going to join in on this particular type of fun, it's worthwhile to understand what it's generally all about.

SL Subculture: An Introduction to Role-Playing

Role-playing, quite simply, is an extended game of Let's Pretend. It's the same state of mind that lets you have fun at a costume party ("I'm Marie Antoinette! Let's eat cake!") or step out of your normal routine when you go on vacation ("What job? I'm a beach bum."). We even used the word *role-play* earlier in this chapter to describe what happens during a Second Life wedding, or the birth of a Second Life baby. Why? Because role-play is all about choosing a scenario, giving everybody a particular part or job to do, and then saying, "go!" The fun isn't in the structure or the "rules," exactly; it's in whatever happens spontaneously after the structure is in place and the rules are set. The more people who join in, the more entertaining and unexpected the group's results will be. Is it any wonder RP is so popular? Seriously—the clothes alone make it worth trying (see Figure 5.15).

FIGURE 5.15 Beautiful, outrageous, amazing clothes for role-playing.

This, in fact, is the key thing to remember about role-players and their communities: They are not, in fact, part of a "subculture" at all. Goths, punks, bikers, dominants and submissives, furries, paranormals, elves, cowboys and sheriffs, crews from starships and pirate ships...the list of Second Life role-players is very, very long. So the math does itself: there are as many residents running around in costume and in character as there are residents who aren't. That means you need to know how to interact with role-players politely if you're not interested in joining in, and intelligently if you want to add yourself into the mix.

So let's talk about this very popular Second Life pastime. If you want to ease into role-playing and try it out, there are ways to do that with minimal effort and time. If you want to jump in with both feet, you can do that, too; there are role-play environments in SL that will be an interesting, fun challenge. On the other hand, if you just want to get a better grasp on who's doing what, the rest of this chapter will be informative for you, too.

Dressing the Part: Role-Playing, Act I

Some role-playing communities in Second Life are fairly wide-open to newcomers. There are few to no extra guidelines involved, other than the Big Six and other stuff in the terms of service agreement.

However, it really helps to be wearing theme-accurate, good-quality gear when you walk up for the first time. If you've taken the time to kit yourself out beforehand, so that you look like a goth, a punk, a biker—or any other sort of role-player—you'll have more credibility. Effort equals genuine interest, across the board, when RP is involved (see Figure 5.16).

FIGURE 5.16 Clothing makes the knight and the pirate.

Generally speaking, there are three types of role-playing communities, above and beyond the population at large that do the RP events already mentioned (weddings, childbirth, etc.). The first type of RP community is the most welcoming and the easiest to approach if you want to join in. These RPers are bikers on Harley Davidsons; punks or goths hanging out in a club that plays that kind of music; and so on. Largely the activity in question is a social one, and you signal your interest in getting involved by dressing the part (see Figure 5.17).

FIGURE 5.17 Hit the open road or the next rave.

If you start up a conversation with someone in these environments, it's probably going to be about general "crossover" topics. For example, you can start up a conversation about a specific motorcycle manufacturer or The Ramones without giving any thought to whether or not that subject is "appropriate" for where you are. This is the other big difference between this first type of role-play and the others two mentioned next: You usually don't have to think about whether or not you're **IC** or **OOC** because it's all the same.

It's also fairly easy to find these sorts of role-playing opportunities. If you're out shopping for a goth skin or Hell's Angels gear, you're quite likely to bump into other residents looking for the same stuff. These are the people who might belong to Groups, or know the clubs and hangouts, where you want to be. So check Profiles, look at titlers, ask about Groups, and strike up conversations. Also keep an eye on the Events calendars for happenings that might suit your interests, and eventually you'll find the social debut you're looking for.

Acting the Part: Role-Playing, Act 2

The second type of role-playing environment gets slightly more intense, but in a good way. Joining in requires a little more concentration on the part of everybody involved and a greater degree of cooperation. The way you dress and the way you ease into the situation matters even more, because "intermediate" role-play in Second Life requires you to modify your behavior.

What constitutes "intermediate-level" role-play? Think about the Wild West as an example. If you've ever seen a Western, you know that the clothes, the language, and some aspects of daily life in that environment are largely familiar. If another role-player in that environment hands you a gun or a butter churn or a deck of cards, you'll know what to do next. You also know the difference between a cowboy, an outlaw, a rancher, a saloon girl, and a sheriff. Furthermore, you probably know enough to say you arrived on the last stagecoach and not the midnight flight from Dulles.

In other words, in an intermediate-level role-play environment, you know enough of "the story" to be able to present yourself convincingly. The key is that the main elements of the story are widely known and understood by a large enough number of average people. Nobody needs to be told, for example, that police are on the side of the victim, that samurai are experts with swords, or that vampires need to drink human blood to survive. So if vampires are part of the "storyline," the average curious resident knows there will be crucifixes, garlic, or holy water involved (see Figure 5.18).

FIGURE 5.18 Vampires, samurai, and doctors— oh my!

Ironically, the greatest strength of an intermediate-level role-playing environment in Second Life is also its greatest weakness. Namely, it's not so difficult to get involved in such an RP community, but it can be hard to keep the ball rolling. You buy your gear, you get involved, you're invited to join the Group. You get deputized, or bitten, or apprenticed to a master swordsman, or signed aboard a ship...and what then? What's next? All too often, momentum dies on an intermediate-level RP SIM because there's too little agreement on the rules, the goal, or even the point.

So what do you do if you find yourself in this situation? If you have the time and the gusto, band together with your comrades and create a more concrete RP framework. Try to figure out what you do and don't find entertaining, and how you could do things differently if you started over. If, for example, you all enjoy a specific TV show, movie, novel, or game that creates the kind of world you also want to create, consider building an homage-type RP environment. This is, in fact, the strategy that many role-players have adopted in order to create a sense of familiarity *and* cohesion.

Accepting the Part: Role-Playing, Act 3

The third and most intricate type of "advanced" role-play in Second Life is a type of online alchemy. These communities have taken a particular theme, imported RP guidelines and expectations from elsewhere, and added in the best features and capabilities of SL. The result—in all three examples mentioned here—has been very successful. Even though the RP is much stricter in terms of the rules each community agrees to follow, they all attract and keep large numbers of participants. This, in turn, stimulates investment of time and energy. Landowners commit entire regions to advanced RP, and designers specialize in costumes and props, which makes it easier for more residents to get curious and get involved. It's the type of self-perpetuating cycle that nobody can plan or force, and for some residents, the allure is irresistible.

The most important pro/con of advanced role-play has to do with its complexity. If you've never read any of John Norman's novels about Gor, for example, you won't know what to expect or really how to behave. In this world of "counter-earth," there's an elaborate caste system, no modern technology to speak of, and a fairly inflexible code of etiquette. There are also plenty of "Goreans" in Second Life who used to role-play Gor elsewhere online via IRC and such. So how do you find your way in, without appearing to be a newcomer?

Naughtiness and Role-Play in Second Life

By now you've probably figured out that "naughtiness" is a synonym for that big elephant in the middle of the virtual living room: sex in Second Life. On the one hand, nobody's able to really ignore it. Sex and sexual behavior are everywhere in SL. Yet on the other, many residents of SL feel strongly about having naughtiness sprung on them. They don't want to see it, hear it, or be propositioned with it unless it's their choice.

If this describes the way you feel, explore role-playing communities with care. Remember that role-playing is all about "let's pretend," and there are lots of people out in the virtual world who are exploring sexual options they won't or can't explore in their real lives. Also realize, though, that nobody taking that particular approach to their Second Life is expecting you to join in—unless you deliberately put your avatar in a certain place at a certain time.

If you're worried about wandering into this type of scenario by mistake, relax. You will almost always, 99.9 percent of the time, have fair warning. The owners of such regions and areas know the rules and they post them—in Search listings, in Profile descriptions, and on notecards that get handed to you automatically once you teleport in. But if you still find yourself in a naughty situation that doesn't interest you, just TP to your home location or exit Second Life. It's tough to remember you have those choices when you get shocked, startled, or offended, but you do.

As a general rule, the "hardcore" role-playing regions in Second Life make Visitor or Observer tags available. Usually, you can't miss them; there are Visitor Detectors throughout such places that will deposit tags into your Inventory along with notecards containing the laws or guidelines. If you are given such items when you arrive on a SIM, don't hesitate. Put on the tag and open the notecard(s). These are tools designed to give you the means and opportunity to join in on the fun immediately and knowledgably.

You can also sit yourself down in a public place—wearing that tag, of course—and observe, observe, observe. Just by taking this time to scout out your surroundings, you will be signaling others that you're curious and thoughtful. More likely than not, these others already in character will respond to you in a friendly way and help you out.

FIGURE 5.19 Elves, Goreans, and Furries: some research required.

It takes patience, forethought, and attention to detail to really get into advanced role-playing. But that's the fun for a lot of people: utterly losing yourself, or freeing a part of yourself, by assuming the identity and culture of someone completely different. Part of the fun of being a furry or an elf, just as two other examples, is in separating yourself from being human. It can be fun, or interesting, or just plain indulgent, to walk around in fur or scales instead of skin for a while (see Figure 5.19).

In the next chapter, you'll begin your tour of building in Second Life—but not just building houses. The tools and menus covered in the next few chapters are the same means to making clothes, jewelry, cars, furniture, water, smoke, and everything else you can see in Second Life. So even if architecture isn't your particular cup of tea, chances are good you'll still find something interesting in the upcoming pages.

ADDITIONAL CREDITS

You can find all the brand, style, color, and designer information on items shown in the figures in the online appendix you get when registering your book at at www.peachpit.com/secondlife. See page v for details.

chapter 6

DESIGNING YOUR HOME

It's a fact of Second Life: The longer you stay, the more interested you become in establishing a home base. Sometimes, the need is social. You want to be able to have friends over and hang out (and impress them with your collection of European sports cars). Sometimes, it's wish fulfillment. You always wanted to live in a log cabin, or a Frank Lloyd Wright house, or the Forbidden Palace, or an underwater grotto. Sometimes, it's also a nesting type of thing—you and your Second Life significant other (or your extended family) want the intimacy of sharing space—building or buying a house, furnishing it together, and so on. The reasons are varied, but the statistics state the obvious: There are far more settlers than wanderers in Second Life. So chances are, someday, you'll want someplace to call your Home Sweet Home.

Residency 101: Options and Possibilities

There are a handful of considerations to keep in mind when you decide to go residence hunting. They are the following:

○ How much money do you want to spend per month in real-life currency?

○ How much space do you need or want?

○ What style of home do you need or want?

○ Do you want to build your house yourself?

○ Is there a specific location that interests you, and if so, why?

Costs and Expenses

In real life, there are two common payment arrangements for housing: You either rent, or you own. In Second Life, it's pretty much the same thing. You can either buy a piece of land for a one-time, large chunk of cash, or you can pay a smaller amount of money once a week or once a month as rent. However, in SL, there's an additional cost known as **tier**. *Tier* is the rough equivalent of a condo association fee, another set amount of money you pay each month. The amount you pay, and to whom who you pay it, depends on where your home is located.

In Chapter 4, we discussed the two types of land in Second Life—mainland property and private island property. If you buy a piece of mainland property, or a whole private island, you'll pay tier to Linden Lab; how much tier depends on the size of the land you bought. However, if you buy private island land from another resident, you are also probably going to pay some sort of tier to them. So there are going to be two costs involved when buying land—the initial investment to purchase the land, and then the monthly tier fee on top of that.

The sizable expense involved in buying is the reason why so many residents choose to rent. If you rent, you avoid jacking up your tier fee because as far as Linden Lab is concerned, you don't own any land. Also, most rental agreements are by the week and not the month. So you don't have to stay financially invested for very long if you decide to move.

You should also consider how much money you want to spend on your home itself. A large lot is nice, but can you also afford a big house? If you spend a lot on the land and the house, do you have enough left for the amount of furniture, rugs, plants, and other stuff to do the house justice? It's easy to get carried away with spending Lindens because you seem to get so much more game

∫Language

tier *n.* Also known as the *land use fee*. Additional money paid to a landowner by buyers and tenants on a monthly basis. Linden charges tier for mainland property, and many resident landlords charge tier for lots on their private islands.

Location, Location, Location

MY FIRST PIECE OF LAND was a lovely spot on part of the first mainland continent. It was bordered by water on two sides, a truly rare find—with a gorgeous Linden-made waterfall spilling into a rocky estuary that dribbled toward the sea. I didn't care how much the property cost (a *lot*). I had to have it. So I coughed up the Lindens and considered myself lucky.

I met my next-door neighbor while I was laying out floorboards. She was wonderfully friendly; we talked about shared interests we saw on each other's Profiles, and I admired her beautiful three-story house.

Then she added casually, "Oh by the way, I'd build your house on the far side of your land if I were you." When I asked why she said, "The casino."

I understood her words, of course, but I didn't understand what she meant. So I built my house, carefully and lovingly, at the center of my land. A week or so later, when I was placing flowers around the edge of my patio, I heard, "WE HAVE A WINNER!" and "SORRY! YOUR NAME DOES NOT BEGIN WITH Q! PLAY AGAIN SOON!" Moments later, I heard the same thing again.

As it turned out, the casino owner was done building, too, and he had begun installing his gambling machines. The machines would "scream" messages in open chat—invitations to play, congratulations for winners, cheery consolations for losers, and on and on. This isn't just obnoxious in principle, either. If you get too close to too many screaming objects, you literally cannot hold a conversation in chat. Everybody's words get lost

in the din, as the Second Life server automatically scrolls them up and out of view to make room for more screaming. All speech on the grid is treated equally.

I learned a couple important lessons, of course. One, read the fine print. Don't move into a mixed zone area if you want peace and quiet. Two, be a snoopy neighbor. I didn't buy my next piece of property until I had flown all the way around it, out to 20 meters circumference (minimum hearing distance). I clicked on every house to get to the Profiles of all my potential neighbors, looking for references to hosting raves or other noisy pastimes. Last but not least, I learned how to use the Link tool and glue my house together into one big piece. That helped make moving out somewhat less of a hassle. But I still had to un-arrange the furniture, pull up all the plants, and start over on a new piece of land. So take it from me: *Caveat emptor* applies to real estate in Second Life, too.

money in exchange for real currency—at this writing, For example, L$1,000 costs roughly $4 U.S. But many, many residents have blown small fortunes on establishing a large and lavish home, only to realize 30 days later that they just couldn't afford it.

Size Matters: Proportional Living Space

If you browse the areas in Search where land and houses are listed, you will find a dizzying array of choices. You can rent a single room in a boarding house. You can buy a condo. You can live in an apartment or a townhouse. You can live in any size, shape, type, and style of house you can imagine—and a couple of types you probably couldn't (see Figures 6.1–6.3).

Regardless of whatever catches your fancy, try to keep a few proportion-related issues in mind when you're choosing your house. First, remember the location of the camera: behind and above you. The dimensions of your dwelling have to accommodate this way of "seeing," or the camera will twitch around to keep up with you.

You should also keep the dimensions of your avatar in mind for similar reasons. A tall and brawny guy will feel confined in a space that feels fine to a shorter, slender woman. Then again, few human-sized living quarters will seem appropriate to "furries," who often only come up to a human woman's shoulder—and enormous avatars like dragons or megamechs won't fit inside a typical house at all.

Minimum Measurements on Room Size

If your avatar of choice is basically human-shaped, there are a few room-related measurement issues you should keep in mind. These defaults always apply, whether you are buying furniture or renting a place to live, or building a house from scratch.

For ease of movement and optimal design, you'll want a minimum ceiling height of four meters. Shorter walls will interfere with the movement of the camera and make you feel uncomfortable as the resident. Taller ceilings are fine, but the overall design effect of the room as a whole might not be as impressive, for example, a glimpse of ceiling completes the "frame" effect of a room.

Similarly, look for rooms that measure 40 square meters or more. That size will sound, and probably look, very large at first. But once you start to walk around it, especially if another resident is with you and the camera swings to follow you, you'll realize the benefit. Also keep in mind that Second Life furniture is oversized by similar proportions, so your stuff won't look right in rooms that are too small, either.

FIGURE 6.1 A floating palace.

FIGURE 6.2 A treehouse.

FIGURE 6.3 Whatever your dream house looks like, you can have it.

Remember Second Life's Build tools measure meters, not feet. Roughly speaking, one meter equals three feet, which is a fairly significant difference in size.

The proximity of other houses or buildings is an additional consideration, because soundproofing does not exist in Second Life. This means that others standing within 20 meters of your avatar can overhear everything you type in open chat, whether or not you can see them. So think twice before choosing apartments with shared walls, townhouses built right on the sidewalk or the street, and small lots of land with no green space between them. (Unless, of course, you're not particularly shy.)

If you're going to indulge in R-rated behavior, keep it discreet. Don't use naughty **poseballs** in plain sight of public space, and don't be explicit in open chat if other residents are or might be close-by. Granted, there are some clubs and such where voyeurism is part of the fun. But, in most areas, it's hugely uncool, and residents do not appreciate the show.

ʃLanguage

poseball *n.* A special object that is scripted to animate your avatar if you click and stand on it. Poseballs are most often gender-specific—pink ones for female animations and blue ones for male animations—but they can come in any color. They are also labeled with brief descriptions of what they "do," but be aware: if you see pink and blue poseballs close together, they are probably naughty or even blatantly kinky. (There's more on using poseballs wisely in Chapter 5, "Designing Your Social Life.")

Skyboxes, Dungeons, and Living Underwater

Not everybody wants to live on terra firma. Skyboxes are probably the most popular type of alternative housing, because the airspace above the ground affords the most privacy. They are also the easiest to build, often little more than a big platform, which even a beginner can construct. Teleporters are highly recommended as a means of getting up and down from skyboxes, though. In-world physics make it impossible for an avatar to fly up to a skybox, without purchasing and using a special flying device.

Dungeons or underground rooms are also popular, but not always practical. The height of mainland property is often preset at or near sea level, which means you cannot always lower the land surface down far enough. On a private island, though, you can dig down much farther, but it doesn't always guarantee privacy. The 20-meter rule applies vertically as well as horizontally, and the ground is not soundproof. So check out any dungeon space very carefully. Take measurements in all directions, and be ready to move on if there's not enough room for comfort or privacy.

Living underwater is definitely an option, too, as avatars cannot drown or float. In fact, some mainland property isn't property at all. It's just open sea, located somewhere near the actual Linden-constructed shoreline, and most owners will use this "land" for skyboxes. But if you find a place at the bottom of the sea, there are two things to remember. First, everything underwater will look blue unless the builder used just the right textures. Also, water isn't soundproof, and boating is a popular pastime, so there's no perfect guarantee of privacy.

Building 101: Doing It Yourself

Here's the scenario: You buy or rent the perfect lot of land. You start looking around at **prefabs**—houses built and sold by other residents—and then you find "The One." It's your dream house, a prefab built by another resident. But, there's one nagging thing wrong.

It might cost too much. It might be too big or the wrong shape for your land. It might use more prims than you can spare. It might be the wrong color, or too dark in color, or it's shingled instead of faced with brick. Then the lightbulb goes off. You don't need to buy your dream house. You can build it, for free, and make it just what you want!

Before you blow your entire budget on furniture, take a deep breath. It's true that you can build just about anything in Second Life. It's also true that many, many fantastic builders learned as they went. But it takes a long time to learn how to use the Build tools, even to make simple things, and you'll have more frustrations than successes.

So, if you're eager to move in and get settled, buy a prefab. If you can wait, and you're determined to live in a dwelling you built yourself, consider the following tricks and techniques as a way to get started.

Remember, the following sections of this chapter are not a complete tutorial on Second Life's Build tools. They are an introduction only, to help you become more familiar with the way objects are constructed. If you want more detailed help and advice, browse the Second Life forums and the Knowledge Base, and do a Search for building-related classes in-world.

The Build Tools: Choosing Shape

Prims, no pun intended, are the basic building blocks of everything in Second Life. There are 13 basic shapes provided, as shown in Figure 6.4.

The first step in any building project is the creation of an object. Click the Build button along the bottom of the Second Life window to open the Build palette and then click the square blue Create button. A plywood box will appear out of thin air—this is the default size, shape, and type of **object** you create with the Build tool.

*ʃ*Language

prefab *n.* A complete, constructed building. Prefabs are completely finished and appear full size when you drag them from your Inventory and place them on the ground. This easy setup is what makes prefabs so popular (and sometimes so expensive).

object *n.* Anything created and placed on the grid. Oftentimes, there's confusion between prims and objects, but think of it like this. "Object" refers to what you created—a chair, for example—which looks like a single thing at a glance. "Prims" are the shape(s) you used to make that object.

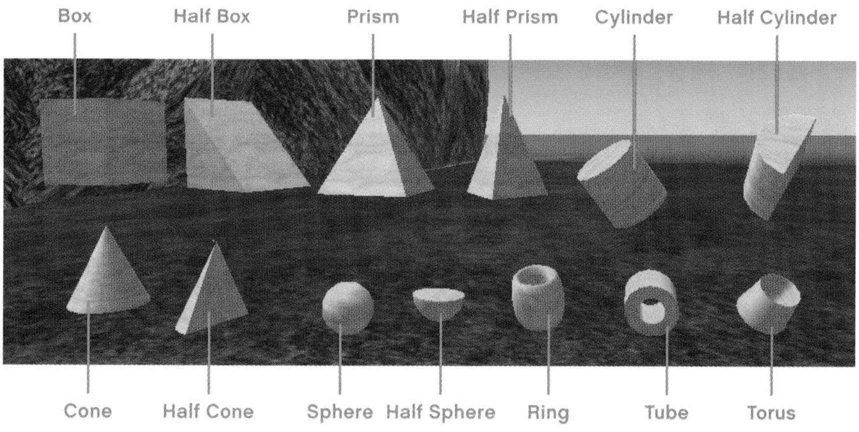

FIGURE 6.4 The 13 basic prims.

Box   Half Box   Prism   Half Prism   Cylinder   Half Cylinder

Cone   Half Cone   Sphere   Half Sphere   Ring   Tube   Torus

Sandboxes: The Best Freebie Ever

If you don't have land yet, or anyplace else to practice building, do a Search for sandboxes. Sandboxes are permanently empty land reserved for public building. You can spend as much time as you want, and build anything you want, with no costs or obligations. However, there is a strict sandbox system of etiquette:

1. Don't bother other builders. Small talk is fine if the other resident hasn't set out any prims yet, but once the building begins, ease off on the conversation—and don't interrupt without a polite apology.

2. Don't test objects that blow smoke, steam, flames, or other floating prims. They are temporarily blinding for everyone around you, too.

3. Don't build, test, bring, or use weapons. Period.

4. Don't peddle things. Residents visit sandboxes to build, not to buy, and "traveling salesmen" are just plain obnoxious.

5. Don't leave your things behind when you're done and go elsewhere. Even though sandboxes are typically set to automatically "wipe" or delete all objects on a regular basis, your stuff will be taking up space somebody else wants to use.

6. This is an addendum to Rule #5: Do not, do not, *do not* use a sandbox as a store or a garbage dump. If you have a few items to sell and you can't afford to rent commercial space, try a yard sale. If you've got something in your Inventory you no longer want or need, delete it and empty the trash.

Take a close look at the object you just made. From this point forward, building becomes a matter of two tasks: making changes to these default type, texture, and shape, and connecting this prim to one or more other prims if needed. That's the nuts and bolts of building in Second Life.

Let's start by making changes.

If you want to work with a different type of prim—something other than a box—you can either a) create the non-box from scratch or, b) change the box to something else. It's easy to get rid of the box, or any object you've created, by right-clicking on it and choosing Delete from the Pie menu.

⇨ Remember to Take Out the Trash

Deleting an object you've created does not make it vanish into the ether. The Second Life grid just moves deleted stuff into your Inventory's Trash folder. These objects will hang around, too, even after you log out of SL, until you select Empty Trash from the File drop-down menu. So it pays to make emptying your Trash a frequent habit.

To create a different type of object from scratch, click the blue Build tool, click the square blue Create icon, and click one of the preset shape options. Then move your mouse to a spot on the ground—the cursor will look like a sparkly wand—and click once. An object shaped like the prim of your choice will appear. Now you can move to the next step: changing either the dimensions or the texture of your object.

Which building task should come first—changing an object's dimensions or changing its texture? It is a matter of opinion, and also a matter of intention. Some builders will texture prims immediately, no matter what their final shape will look like. This is certainly wise if you are making something very small, like chain links or eyelashes. But it's not necessary if the prim is going to stay fairly large and easy to edit. Also, if you are building something that is going to be fully or partially transparent, like glass or water, it's easier to work with solid-looking prims until they are sized and positioned perfectly.

The Build Tools: Changing Size

When you create an object, three sets of orientation tools appear at the same time, in red, blue, and green. We'll talk about how to use these tools to move objects a little later on in this chapter. For now, you'll be using them as reference markers to adjust the object's dimensions. So click the blue Build button at the bottom of the Second Life window to open the Build palette, create a box, and then click the square blue Edit button.

General Design Advice: Megaprims, Temp-Rezzers, and Exploits

There are items available in Second Life, and mentioned in the forums, that will enable you to work around the basic constraints imposed on prims. Some of these clever inventions used to be on the edge of kosher, used at a resident's own risk, until Linden Lab gave these items the nod. The most popular of these are mega prims and temp-rezzers (defined below). However, there are also items and even techniques called *exploits:* things that take advantage of a bug or other yet-unsolved problem with the grid. Exploits are considered violations of the Terms of Service agreement and using them may result in serious consequences.

A mega prim is a single-prim object (such as a sphere) that is larger in one or all dimensions than 10 meters. Some of them measure the equivalent of a handful of 10m × 10m prims. The largest mega prims are enormous: big enough to cover an entire 65,536 sq/m private island with a single, perfectly flat, rectangular surface. That explains the benefit of mega prims very clearly: you can save yourself dozens or hundreds of regular-sized prims by using just one that's mega-size.

A temp-rezzer (short for *temporary resolver*) is scripted to change the way the grid displays an object. Most objects created by residents are permanent, and the grid determines whether or not it can support more prims in a given area by keeping count of what's permanent. So a temp-rezzer works by changing an object's type from permanent to temporary, forcing the grid to re-resolve it repeatedly and making the object "worth" zero prims. The appeal of this work-around is obvious, too.

However, there are only certain situations in which Linden Lab allows residents to use mega prims and temp-rezzers. Mega prims are not considered legal on the mainland at this time; they are only permitted on private island property. Temp-rezzers are universally allowed in objects that shoot things like arrows or bullets, or emit dissipating effects like smoke or confetti. But you can also use temp-rezzers to change a building, or tree, or something else that should be permanent. So why would anybody go without these work-arounds if Linden Lab permits them? The answer is *risk*. Any time you use just one mega prim, or one temp-rezzer, you are forcing the grid to work just a little bit harder in a way it was not necessarily designed to function. The result of this demand is wildly unpredictable; some regions are covered in mega prims and have no trouble, but others incorporate just one or two and crash routinely. Temp-rezzers are especially notorious for creating crash cycles, even when used in small numbers. This is a situation where the grid repeatedly tries and fails to rez an entire region, and no one but a Linden Lab employee can fix the problem. This is why some residents forego mega prims, temp-rezzers, and other new SL technologies; they'd rather spend the prims and have greater stability.

It's logical to assume that this type of evolution of SL will continue—residents will keep tinkering with the code, tools, and features. Some of these inventions will be embraced and made acceptable for everybody to use. But other creations might not stand up to scrutiny or support testing on the grid at large. So be careful what you do and build if you're out there on the edge of the Second Life envelope. Some "new and improved" work-arounds won't deliver what they promise—and if you go too far, your account could be terminated for ToS violations.

The tools you want are on the Object tab page, in the lower-left corner—Size and Rotation, broken out into three text boxes apiece (see Figure 6.5). The X-, Y-, and Z-axes are color-coordinated to the orientation tools hovering around and near the box. So, for example, if you increase the Z setting in the Size box from 0.500 to 1.00, the box will double in height.

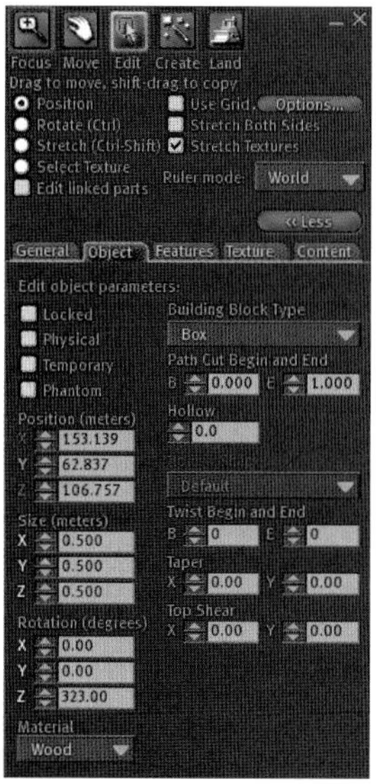

Just below the Size settings are the Rotation text boxes. If you're having flash-backs to Geometry class, you're on the right track—change the X setting from 0.00 to 45.00, and the box will spin around.

Linden Lab designed other settings/measurements in Second Life to cor-respond to red, green, and blue as well. If you look at the top edge of the SL window, you'll see three numbers labeled X, Y, and Z. This is the position of your avatar on the grid, relative to the size of the land under your feet. So you should get used to identifying red, green, and blue numbers with grid-related information; it's universal, consistent association throughout the Second Life interface.

There are many other options and tweak tools on this tab page. But for now let's move on to texturing and save the intermediate building options for later.

The Build Tools: Applying Texture

If you take another close look at Figure 6.4, you can see how ambient light in Second Life plays on an object's surface. There's not much you can do to affect the quality or hue of the light in SL, but you can drastically affect the appear-ance of objects with textures. If you change the texture on an object, you can transform more than its surface pattern. You can use textures to work with in-world physics to trick the eye in all kinds of clever ways.

Just to keep it simple, for now we're going to focus on the Texture and Color display boxes and the Repeats Per Face tools. (We'll come back to the other choices here in later chapters.)

The default settings for texture and color are showing in Figure 6.6. The default texture setting is this blond plywood; the default color is white; the default repeat settings are a height and a width of 1, with the Flip option left unchecked. You can see from studying this tab page, even before you start experimenting, that it's easy to make both dramatic changes and subtle tweaks. This is the curse and the blessing of all the Build tools; they are so multifaceted that they can be overwhelming.

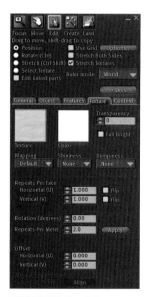

FIGURE 6.5 The Edit > Object tab page in the Build palette.

FIGURE 6.6 The Edit > Texture tab page in the Build palette.

For starters, let's play with the color only.

Using the Color Picker dialog box (see Figure 6.7), you can choose colors precisely with the RGB settings near the upper-left corner, or generally with the eyedropper tool near the bottom center. There are 32 color "chips" that enable you to save colors you particularly like. Whenever you select a color, it will temporarily appear in the Current Color viewing window. You can save the color appearing there by dragging and dropping it onto one of the "chips." Click Select to save all your choices and changes.

This is what the default plywood-type texture can look like if you simply play with color and transparency (see Figure 6.8).

It's easy to make the wood look colorwashed or stained, if the color is pale enough and the texture is dark enough. You can also cover up the plywood look altogether with a medium or darker shade to create a chunk of smooth, solid color. (The "recipes" for all these color effects are listed in the online appendix.)

The exception to this method is for producing white as a solid color. When you see white displayed in the Color window on the Edit > Texture tab page, the Second Life grid has set the actual color to nothing. So the only way to get a solid white box, in this instance, is to click the Texture window and click the blue Blank button.

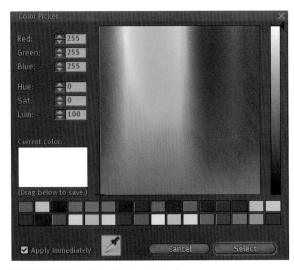

FIGURE 6.7 The Color Picker dialog box.

FIGURE 6.8 Adding various colors to the same texture.

To add a texture to an object, click the Texture window on the Edit > Texture tab page. The Pick: Texture dialog box will appear (see Figure 6.9). Texture options can be found in a number of places, not just the actual Textures folder in your Inventory. If you buy a set of textures, they might be dropped into your Inventory in the Objects folder, or right alongside the Objects folder at the same level in the tree. You can add snapshots from the Photo Album, and you can also find free textures from Linden in the Library folder (see Figure 6.10).

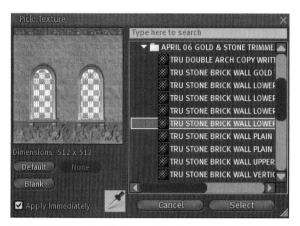

FIGURE 6.9 The Pick: Texture dialog box.

FIGURE 6.10 Free textures provided by Linden in your Library > Textures folder.

To start, click down through your Inventory folders until you find the textures you want and click them once. The big square window near the top-left corner of the Pick: Texture dialog box is a preview window. You can browse textures here only, or you can also check the Apply Immediately check box at the bottom-left corner and see textures temporarily applied to your object.

After you've found the texture you want, click Select, and the Pick: Texture dialog box will close. Now you can refine the texture you just selected. You can repeat the texture up to 100 times in either direction, horizontally or vertically, to create stripes, a tile effect, or a soft blurry color blend. However, some textures created by residents were designed to be used at the default 1-to-1 setting. Figure 6.11 on the next page shows some examples.

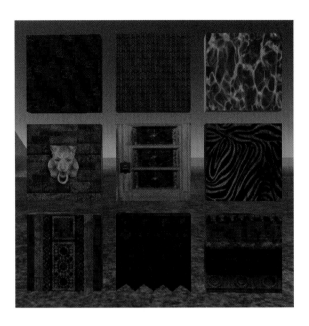

FIGURE 6.11 Textures created and sold by Second Life residents.

These designs will give you an idea of just how much a single texture can add to your creations. There's a lot more you can do with textures, the simple ones and the more complex. We will get to advanced texture usage in Chapter 7, "Designing Your Homestead" and Chapter 8, "Designing Your Empire." In the meantime, once objects are sized and textured, it's time to position them in place.

The Build Tools: Finishing Up

When you create an object, three sets of orientation tools appear at the same time, in red, blue, and green. You can activate these tools by right-clicking or Apple-clicking on any object you created. After that, you can push or pull the object by grabbing these tools; right-click on them if you're using a PC or Apple-click if you're using a Mac. The larger arrows, connected by thin matching lines, are for moving the object freehand. The smaller triangular-shaped "handles" will move the object in measured increments along a grid.

Aligning two objects precisely is also a matter of math. For example, if you want to set two one-meter boxes side-by-side to make a seamless single object, use the three X, Y, and Z Position measurements. Choose one box, select it, and open the Edit > Object tab page to look at the Position measurements. You want to cut and paste the Z-axis measurement first, from the first box into the Z Position window of the second box. This will ensure that both boxes are aligned vertically. Repeat this process with the X-axis measurement, so the boxes are also aligned horizontally.

The Y-axis measurements, however, will not be identical. The Y-axis measurement of the box on the right needs to be exactly one meter higher than the Y-axis measurement of the box on the left. This difference accounts for the exact width of the box on the right. So now, when you cut and paste in these numbers, the boxes will be precisely aligned in all three directions.

There are two ways to connect two objects together into one. First, you select one object, hold down the Shift key, click on the other object(s) to select it/them as well, and then choose Link from the Tools drop-down menu. This action will glue the objects together, until or unless you select it and choose Tools > Unlink.

You can also select a much larger group of aligned prims if you click the blue Build button to open the Build palette and then click the square blue Edit button. Now you can hold down the right mouse key, or the Apple-click combination, and draw a rectangle in the air over the top of all the prims you want to link. Every prim you've grabbed will be outlined in glowing blue; then choose Link from the Tools drop-down menu. This action will glue the objects together, until or unless you select it and choose Tools > Unlink.

The Build Tools: A Demonstration

To finish up the introduction to Second Life's Build tools, let's take a walk through a simple demonstration: a simple Cape Cod type, two-story house. This group of 12 prims is going to form the basic building blocks for the whole house. The math involved in lining all these prims up is fairly simple, and it's easy to visualize the final product (see Figure 6.12).

FIGURE 6.12 Plywood floors and walls: the beginnings of a house.

These textures are part of a set that includes plain walls, walls with windows, a door texture, and also a roof texture. Individual textures sold in sets are perfectly matched and coordinated by design (see Figure 6.13 on the next page for an example). So you can mix them and experiment with them confidently, and also add little details like shutters, windows, and flowerboxes without using up prims.

Once you've positioned all the pieces and added texture, it's time to lock everything in place. The easiest way to Link a whole building together is to fly up, scoot over, and look down with the Camera Control tools. Go into Mouselook

FIGURE 6.13 A matched texture set: the easiest way to build windows and details.

(press Escape and then the M key) so that your view will be completely unobstructed, and then click-drag-select all the pieces of the house to Link them.

The easiest way to create a duplicate of anything you've made, whether it's a single-prim or a multi-prim object, is click-drag-copy it. Select the object(s) by clicking and choosing Edit from the Pie menu. Then grab the large arrow that points in the direction you want to position the duplicate, hold down the Shift key, and click-and-drag the arrow. An exact copy will appear above, below, or beside the original. In Figure 6.14, this is how the second floor was created.

FIGURE 6.14 A time-saving trick: the click-drag-copy maneuver.

FIGURE 6.15 The finishing touches: a roof, a door, and you're done.

The total prim count on this whole house, once it's completed with the final added bits, as shown in Figure 6.15, is just 31 prims. This house is a good size, shape, and prim cost for your first piece of land especially. The footprint of the house also leaves enough room for some landscaping and even a patio or a pool.

Now that you've walked through all the fundamental tasks involved in building, all you need to perfect your technique is time and courage. Second Life is the ideal place to learn by doing, and wild experimentation is not just encouraged, but applauded. So set aside some more time to play around in a sandbox, look around in texture stores, and make plenty of educational mistakes. If you stick with it, you'll be amazed at what you can create, even with a small number of prims. The prefabs shown in Figure 6.16 are all considered "starter houses," and look at how different they are from one another.

> ### ADDITIONAL CREDITS
>
> You can find all the brand, style, color, and designer information on items shown in the figures in the online appendix you get when registering your book at at www.peachpit.com/secondlife. See page v for details.

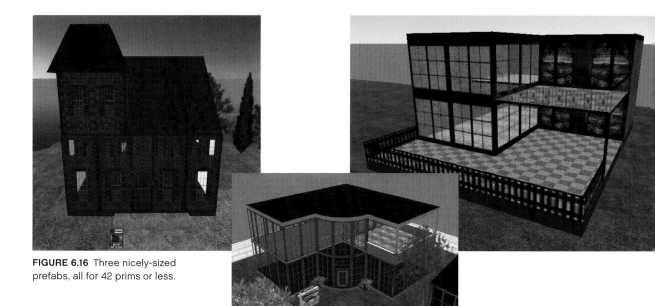

FIGURE 6.16 Three nicely-sized prefabs, all for 42 prims or less.

chapter 7

DESIGNING YOUR HOMESTEAD

Do you dream of towers and domes? Do you wish for a fountain or a koi pond? What about the design of your greenspace in general—do you want something beyond a plain, flowerless lawn?

This is the chapter to reference when it's time to upgrade. There's advice on selling your first piece of land and shopping intelligently for something bigger. There's an introduction to curved, rounded construction elements for adding visual interest. But first, we will talk a little theory to explain the whys and wherefores of landscaping and microclimate. Then we'll create a few home-and-garden examples.

Here's the key question, though: Is garden envy a good enough reason to start shopping for land again? How much do you have to build, spend, and plant to create something really nice? Fear not—this chapter is also about moderation. So let's get started with more information on Second Life real estate.

Outgrowing Your First Piece of Land

There are a few signs that it's time to consider selling your land and scouting out someplace new. If you get interested in creating, say, vintage motorcycles, then you'll need a "workshop" built on land that gives you enough extra prims to play with. You might also want to consolidate your efforts, space, and other resources efficiently, and build a store or showroom on the same land as your house. For that matter, what if you start collecting vintage motorcycles? You won't want to keep them in your Inventory. You'll want to show them off. So in this scenario, you've got to have enough square meterage to build a nice garage or driveway, and enough prims to let you set out all your treasures.

There also comes a time when residential areas start to "turn over," as Real-tors would say. When a new private island appears, landowners will frequently offer many small lots of land (they make more profit that way). The first wave of residents may be the least wealthy who can only afford the single small lot. But subsequent new tenants buy bigger lots with enough room to put in trees, grass, and flowers. This expansion makes the area look more like a neighbor-hood and less like a mass of tiny box houses.

So the price of the land starts to rise, along with its aesthetic value. The price of your land also starts to rise, especially if your immediate neighbors put their land up for sale. If you set your lot for sale, too, then some fortunate buyer will see two lots he or she can likely join up into one.

Outgrowing Land: Setting a Sale Price

When you've decided to pack up and move up, you must first establish the fair market value of your land. There are two easy ways to do so. First, while you're at home, click the blue Map button near the bottom-right corner of the Second Life window. This will bring up the Map dialog box (see Figure 7.1).

The Map is a top-down view of the area where you are located, plus all eight areas that border it. Land that is set for sale will appear bright yellow with a green dollar sign. If you double-click on any such lot and then click the blue Teleport button, you can visit that exact location and look at the lot. To view the price and other details about the lot, right- or Apple-click on the land itself, and choose Edit Land to open the About Land dialog box (see Figure 7.2).

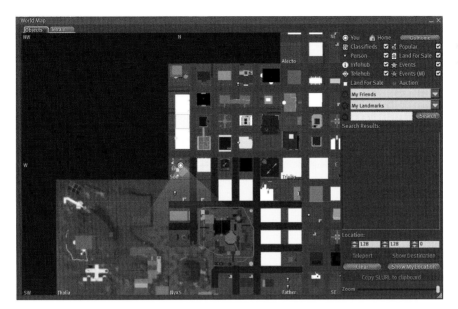

FIGURE 7.1 The Map dialog box: a bird's-eye view of your current location in Second Life.

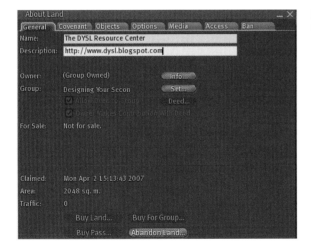

FIGURE 7.2 The About Land dialog box.

In this tab window, the price of the land is displayed in Lindens, and the size of the land is indicated as "Area." You can use this information on other lots on the same SIM as yours to set your sale price. Divide the asking price by the square meterage; for example, if you have a lot that measures 2,560 sq/m, and the asking price is L$50,000, then your asking price would be L$19 per square meter.

Try to visit all lots for sale in the same area as yours, especially if your lot is on the edge of the SIM or on the mainland coast. "Oceanfront" property is always in demand, especially if there's no way for anyone to boat past or build something out in the water that would obstruct the view. Corner lots are also highly desirable—they have twice the view—and are worth a few extra Lindens per square meter.

You should also browse the Land Sales tab page in Search. There's a special search feature near the upper-left corner of the dialog box window that enables you to search by lot size. Type in the square meterage of your land and click the box to check/select it. This will limit search results to all listings that are advertising land for sale of the same size as yours.

Ultimately, you can set any sale price that you want. Set it to the average of other lots for sale or slightly higher to be in line with the current market. Or set it slightly lower to get rid of the land right away. A good general, non-extortionist rule of thumb seems to be taking the price you paid for the land and adding anywhere from 15% to 20%. However, there are plenty of land "**flippers**" out there who are charging 25% more and slightly higher, so it all depends on how much profit you want to make.

Outgrowing Land: Buying Big(ger)

If you've set your land for sale already, chances are pretty good that a) you've determined you can afford a bigger piece of land, and b) you've already got a general idea of what you want next in terms of size, location, and land type. However, we'll run through all those reasons here just in case.

The size of your land is probably going to be determined by your wallet rather than your ambitions. So the same general warnings still apply: Consider the outright purchase price, the monthly tier, and also any decorating-type costs. From this point forward, though, we're going to assume that you've got the strong desire to build, and that you'll want to take the time to fuss with prims until you're cross-eyed.

For the purposes of making examples, we're going to proceed with this chapter as if you went out and acquired 4,096 square meters of land. Generally speaking, this is a nicely sized lot with a fairly generous minimum prim allotment (937 prims) that suits just about everybody. It's also a good working size for

∫Language

flipping *n.* A term borrowed from real-life real estate slang. Flipping involves buying a property for sale, only to turn around and sell it immediately for a higher price, just to make some additional cash. This behavior has been very common throughout Second Life for about a year and a half, causing the price of land to skyrocket and creating sticker shock for most incoming new residents. Logically, also, flipping has pushed many residents to purchase their own private island SIM instead. We will cover the process of buying islands in more detail in Chapter 8, "Designing Your Empire."

demonstrating how landscaping works, and how to make the most of whatever prim "allowance" you've set aside to create your greenspace.

Building, The Sequel: Curvy Shapes

The most popular type of home in Second Life might be an angular, boxy American modern dwelling. But the second most popular type is definitely the gothic castle, complete with towers, turrets, and other architectural features that require an understanding of curvy prims. So let's build ourselves a modest demesne, medieval style, complete with an appropriate garden.

Building Without Corners: Cylinders

To start off, here is a broken-down version of the castle we'll be using for this chapter—a simple modified box with four cylinders sitting on a "stone floor." (see Figure 7.3). Notice that the cylinders are hollowed out and sliced open on the sides adjacent to the center. You can do this to any type of prim by using the Hollow and the Path Cut settings. These tools are located on the Object tab page of the Build window along the right side. Click the blue Build button at the bottom of the Second Life window and then click the square blue Edit icon to get to the correct page (see Figure 7.4).

Don't Do It!

Don't trust your eyes to determine how much land you need. If your first lot of land was 1,536 square meters or less, you could stand in the middle, pan around, and get a realistic sense of what would fit. But once you exceed that size, the "draw distance" factor will trick your eyes, especially if the land is all one texture, such as grass or sand. So how can you make a reliable estimate? Look at different prefabs and take time to walk through the ones you like. Ask the builder(s) about minimum land requirements for the designs you prefer, and narrow down your land search based on your findings.

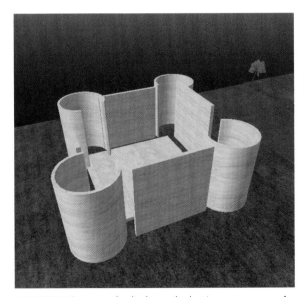

FIGURE 7.3 Boxes and cylinders—the basic components of any castle.

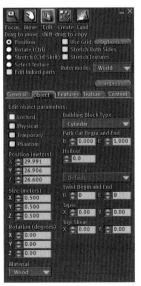

FIGURE 7.4 The Build dialog box, Edit > Object tab page.

Are You a Building Addict (Yet)?

IF YOU ANSWER "yes" to more than one of the following questions, you've got the disease, all right. The real question is...do you even want to be cured?

1. You see prim shapes in the way real-life buildings were constructed.
2. You wish you could renovate your bathroom by using Select > Delete.
3. You've taken a picture of something in your house and imported it as a texture.
4. You pass on a real $10 pillow so you can spend L$2,500 on a virtual couch instead.
5. You've looked at any gigantic monument—Monticello, Topkapi Palace, the biggest pyramid at Giza—and told yourself, "I could build that."

To make a prim hollow, change the Hollow value to any number between 1 and 95; the larger this number, the larger the hollowed-out area will be. As soon as you press Enter (or Return), the middle section of the prim will vanish, leaving behind a vertical "hole." Conversely, notice that the "wall" of the tower gets progressively thinner if you increase the Hollow value. For purposes of building this castle, we want to leave the wall quite thick. So the Hollow value is set at 80. If you need a little more room inside the tower as a result, you can increase the diameter a little bit to make up space.

By default, the hollow section will be the same shape as the prim itself, for example, a cube will have a cube-shaped opening, a cylinder will have a cylindrical opening, and so on. You can change this default setting with the Hollow Shape pull-down menu; the optional, differently shaped opening choices are circle, square, or triangle.

To cut down the side of the cylinder-tower, use the Path Cut tool. The default setting—with 0 in the Begin box and 1 in the End—describes an uncut shape. To slice open the side, change the Begin value to 2 and then to 3. The larger the number value in the Begin box, the larger the opening in the side of the cylinder.

Building Without Corners: Cones

After you link all these pieces together (see Figure 7.5), it's time to put on the roof. You can (and could) always use solid prims to top off your builds, because there's no advantage to using hollow prims when you are looking at the outside roofline. However, from a design point of view, hollow prims can often be used to create beautifully decorated, vaulted ceilings. You can accomplish this two-for-one design strategy by using two different textures on a single one-prim object.

FIGURE 7.5 The pieces of the castle, joined together and ready to be linked.

We will use one of the cone-shaped tower roofs to illustrate using multiple textures. When you first create the cone with the Build > Create tool, it appears pointed end up. To reach the underside more easily, tip the cone on its side; click the blue square Edit icon, click the Rotate radio button, and change the Rotation text box setting to 270. Next, enlarge it so you can see your work: make it 8 × 8 × 4 meters. Now, hollow out the cone by changing the Hollow text box setting to 90. You've ended up with a roof-shaped part that resembles a short, thick ice cream cone with three sides: the outside, the inside, and the flat circular bottom edge.

We want to make the inside of the cone look like wood, and the outside of the cone look like shingles. To apply textures to just one side of an object, right- or Apple-click the object you want to texture, click the blue square Edit icon, and then click the Select Texture radio button. Now click the edge or side of the object where you want to apply a texture; the white "tile marks" for texturing will only appear on the edge or side you are working with. You can select a texture using the Texture tab page and the Pick: Texture dialog box settings.

In this example, we've chosen a wood texture to create a rich, paneled ceiling look, which is historically accurate for medieval European castle design (see Figure 7.6).

If you repeat the process, but select the outside of the cone instead, you can now apply a roofing texture. You won't undo or mistakenly retexture the inside of the cone, as long as the white tile marks only appear on the outside surface. Figure 7.7 shows the finished cone with nicely distressed shingles appearing on the roof side.

When you are working with textures like the ones in this example—both the wood paneling and the shingles—you can alter the effect of each texture quite dramatically by using the Repeats Per Face tool. The example house in the last chapter, and the walls of the castle in this chapter, both use textures at a 1-to-1 ratio. This one copy of the texture fits each side of the wall object perfectly, both vertically and horizontally.

The Repeats Per Face tool allows you to change this horizontal/vertical relationship. In this example of the tower ceiling-roof piece, the vertical repeat will have the most impact on the overall design. On the inside, where the texture creates an illusion of rich detail, you want the wood grain and faux molding to be recognizable. On the outside of the ceiling-roof piece, you want the same thing—the individual shingles should look like shingles. In both situations, relative size is important.

FIGURE 7.6 Texturing just one surface of a single prim: a paneled tower ceiling.

FIGURE 7.7 Texturing just one surface of a single prim: a weathered, shingled roof.

Relative distance is also important, though. The ceiling should look correct from the floor below, where the avatar looking at it will be just a few meters away. The roof shingles, however, will be viewed from a distance. So you want to adjust the vertical repeat in such a way as to make roofing textures look too large from up close. This strategy helps guarantee that they will look just right from the ground below.

➡ General Design Advice: Textures

To get the most out of textures, ignore the descriptions and study what they look like. Water can look like cloth, and vice versa. You can use the Repeats Per Face tool to turn a door into paneling for your dining room, or a fence pattern into a screened window. If a wall texture has decorative trim along the floor that you'd rather have along the ceiling, use the Flip setting to rotate it. The longer you look at a texture, and the longer you experiment with Second Life's Build tools, the more use you can get out of the same single texture design.

Beyond Building: Landscaping in Second Life

Once you have enough land for room, enough prims to spare, and your house design of choice for inspiration, you can really let loose with the green. Not money, but plants—trees, vines, flowers, shrubs, and the most perfect weed- and maintenance-free grass you'll ever find. Landscaping in Second Life is the art of placing plants to create a backdrop for everything else. Many residents will skip landscaping because it does require prims; we'll explain the reason why good-looking plants can (but don't have to) be prim-costly. But ultimately, the best landscaping design is like the perfect application of makeup—if it does its job, landscaping is the finishing touch that calls attention to everything else but itself.

Landscaping 101: What's the Plan?

In Second Life, you can fall in love with landscaping just as easily and rapturously as you can fall in love with building. So before you splurge on too many plants, going overboard in terms of real-life expense and in-world usefulness, devise a strategy. Ask yourself the following questions:

○ **How much land will you really want to set aside for landscaping?**

Walk all the way around your house and look at how much bare land is available on all four sides. Will you want this space to multitask as a deck, patio, porch, gazebo, or some sort of other, detached structure? Do you need walkways or stepping stones, statues, a swimming pool, or some other functional element that should be put in place first?

○ **How many prims do you want to spend?**

Generally speaking, residents tend to spend more prims on their living space and fewer on landscaping. If this is you, don't despair; you can make a nice visual statement with a handful of well-placed trees and a couple rectangular objects textured to look like a box hedge. On the other hand, you can go in the total opposite direction, too: build the Hanging Gardens of Babylon on the ground for fun, and float a skybox for living space somewhere up in the clouds.

○ **Do you want or need a border?**

Sometimes, you want a fence or wall around your property—for ambiance, for blocking out your neighbors' bad design choices, or even to help keep strangers out. All these factors will determine the type, height, thickness, and position of the border. But you can choose the texture or any additional decoration, such as ivy, moss, or climbing flowers.

○ **What will the ground texture look like?**

Even within the fantastical world of Second Life, some landscaping choices will just look illogical and therefore silly. For example, you wouldn't plant a cactus on a green grass lawn, you wouldn't find rosebushes flowering underwater, and palm trees wouldn't survive in the snow.

We're going to use our castle as the property needing a good landscaping, so we are going to proceed with landscaping strategies and choices that would be appropriate for our castle's real-world location.

Landscaping 101: A Quick Overview

Some aspects of real-life landscaping are mercifully absent from Second Life. You'll never have to water, weed, mow, trim, or fertilize. The only common "bugs" are delicate butterflies. You can even have birdsong without nests in the eaves or white splats on the deck. It's a gardening heaven.

The general rules for landscaping design still apply, though not precisely in the same way. In real life, there's no such thing as draw distance, and in Second Life there's no such thing as peripheral vision. So the individual elements involved in SL landscaping have to multitask in a very different way from actual real-life plants and gardens.

As in real life, there are three overarching principles involved in creating a really good landscape design in Second Life. These principles are proportion, transition, and unity—but as with everything real that's been imported into SL, the definition and use of these ideas is slightly different.

Proportion is all about size and scale. In real life, proportion is real simple. Small yards need small plants; big yards need big plants. In Second Life, your yard or garden actually benefits from both. Why? Because in Second Life, simply put, people fly around. You yourself have been encouraged to do so, earlier on in this chapter, when shopping for land. This fact means that you can, and should, capitalize on the view of your land from about 100 feet in the air (see Figure 7.8).

FIGURE 7.8 Looking down on a lovely garden.

In real-life landscaping, transition is all about marrying different sections of a yard or garden. Transition uses the right plants, the right materials, and the right proportions to move people through a space comfortably and pleasingly. In Second Life, most people can't afford enough land, or set aside enough prims, to landscape on such a large scale. So transition in a Second Life yard or garden becomes a matter of trying to cope with design choices other people make that you can't control.

Unity, the third guiding principle, is the same idea/sensation in both real life and Second Life. It describes the overall effect of the finished product, the sense of flow and harmony that a really well-planned garden can evoke. You feel it when you see it. You know it's missing when it's not there. You want to go back again and again, even in Second Life, if you find a garden that has it. Furthermore, if you create a garden with unity, your neighbors will thank you for making the whole region look more attractive. You'll also get lots of visitors, which can be a good thing if you're trying to make money.

So how can you achieve proportion, transition, and unity with landscaping in Second Life? Let's learn a few more vocabulary words, and get started on the yard surrounding our little castle, to find out.

Landscaping 101: Designing the Hardscape

Hardscape is another real-life landscaping term that imports usefully into Second Life. The hardscape also sets the garden's boundaries in terms of square meterage to work with. It makes limitations in terms of texture and color choice; and it also suggests how to group flowers, plants, and trees for maximum effect. Components of the hardscape would include the house, fences and patios, and pathways, sculpture, and fountains.

The Second Life hardscape is slightly different. It also includes everything listed previously, and all similar constructions, such as walls, decks, and statues. But in SL, the hardscape also suggests a frame that surrounds a resident's view of the garden. This includes the ground because it is flat and singly textured by default; typically, you may not have a choice about what type of ground you have to work with.

Our little castle actually provides a very nice hardscaping foundation because it's relatively simple in design. There's little difference in the appearance of each of its four sides. As a castle, it doesn't naturally beg for the addition of things

ſLanguage

hardscape *n.* A carryover term from real-life landscaping. The hardscape is everything in a garden area that doesn't grow. Unlike real life, you can manipulate and retexture your garden's hardscape very quickly and easily. But you can't do anything about what your neighbors have done with their gardens or houses. So hardscaping in Second Life is still somewhat similar to real life.

like a brick patio or screened-in porch. This lack of extensions or add-ons leaves more greenspace to work with than other house styles might have.

Design-wise, a castle does suggest certain parameters for the look of the rest of the garden. A Jacuzzi would look out of place, but a nice marble fountain would not. Stone as a material, generally speaking, would be a good choice for a border wall, a pathway, and even for benches. You could even use the castle as an excuse to go truly purist with your garden design. Replicate an actual/historical garden that exists in real life, around or behind an actual/historical castle. Or challenge yourself even further by using only plants, trees, and flowers typically used in medieval castle gardens.

➡ General Design Advice: Fences, Walls, and Good Neighbors

There's really no such thing as a secure wall in Second Life. Even if flying is disabled in a particular region (something a land owner can choose to do), there are still attachments and other gadgets that allow avatars to jump very high and very far. You can also use the Camera Controls to pan through a wall, select any object on the other side, and use Sit Here on the Pie menu to yank yourself through. Most residents will respect a wall that they cannot see through or over, especially if there's any sort of gate or door. But sadly, if somebody really wants to invade your privacy, you can't count on real-world physics to keep that person out.

Landscaping 101: Choosing Plants and Trees

Shopping for plants, trees, and flowers in Second Life is nothing but fun. In real life, plants have an annoying tendency to behave naturally. You have to water, trim, and coddle them, and there's still every chance they won't bloom. In SL, the only thing that can kill or maim a plant is an Edit tool. No wonder some residents turn into diehard SL gardeners!

Form, line, color, and texture are all staples of real-life landscaping design that also carry over into Second Life. These are terms real-life landscapers use to discuss the appearance and other characteristics of individual plants, trees, and flowers. In terms of Second Life, there are a few extra considerations, too. So let's talk about each of these qualities, and how they can help guide your selection process, before you go out shopping (see Figures 7.9–7.10).

Form, for example, is all about the difference between a Christmas tree and a weeping willow. You certainly can plant these two trees side by side, but would

FIGURE 7.9 A classic color combination; pink, yellow, white, and magenta.

FIGURE 7.10 A classic color combination; yellow, violet, and orange.

FIGURE 7.11 A classic color combination; red, pink, and lavender.

FIGURE 7.12 A classic color combination; white, yellow, and orange.

the end result look good? Not really. The severe lines of the pine tree contrast too sharply against the flowing silhouette of the willow tree, even in SL where all things are possible.

In real-life landscaping, line is about leading the eye from plant to plant, or element to element, in such a way that adds to the overall experience of seeing the whole garden. In Second Life, the idea of line also has to do with technical considerations, such as draw distance and resolution. Line is about designing your SL yard or garden in such a way that lures residents to come closer and wait for everything to rez so they can see the whole thing.

Color and texture in Second Life landscaping are also, partly, about dealing with technical issues. On the one hand, many residents who look at your garden will have fast connections and excellent graphics cards. So what you've planted will quickly rez, and your landscaping will appear as you intended. In this scenario, texture matters because somebody will actually get to see it. On the other hand, there are many residents in SL who try to make do with slow connections, bad lag, and other technical albatrosses. For them, the finer details take too long to rez or never appear at all. All your plants, trees, and flowers will look blurry, so color matters most (see Figures 7.11–7.12).

When you're out shopping for plants, there's one more consideration you should think about—and fortunately, you can do this with a glance. Remember, there's no such thing as peripheral vision in Second Life, so the relative height of every object is very important. That is, how much of a plant, tree, or flower will be visible within the Second Life window when someone is standing nearby?

How to Build Plants in Second Life

Every green thing in Second Life, from single flowers to enormous trees, is constructed the same way. A picture of a plant, flower, or tree is sketched or photographed, and cleaned up using software (Adobe Photoshop and Corel Paint Shop Pro are most popular). The "clean" areas are rendered transparently, leaving just the image of the flower or tree. Then, after the image is imported into Second Life, it is applied to a thin rectangular prim as a texture. Multiple copies of this prim are placed at precise 90-degree angles to one another, intersecting at the center to form a sort of asterisk. If this positioning process is done correctly, using three or more prims, a fairly realistic three-dimensional "plant" will result.

If you take the time to wander around garden centers in Second Life, you'll notice that greenery falls into two height categories. This might sound redundant, but plantable things are sized to be entirely visible up-close, or to run far off the edge of the Second Life window. The reason has to do with transition and line. Ideally, you want to design a garden or lawn that first draws the eye to what's right there, and then suggests there's more to see beyond the "frame" of the SL window.

Plantable things for "right there" will generally come in four heights: to the knee, to the waist, to the shoulder, and at or near the top of the head. Plantable things that run off the edge of the Second Life window are going to be many meters taller—trees, shrubs, and climbing greenery running up an arbor or the walls of a building. By mixing and matching "right there" plantables, you can direct someone's eye to the best features of your property. Similarly, well-positioned plants and flowers of differing heights will camouflage or even fool the eye when it passes over the worst features.

You really need to buy one plantable of each height, even if you have a small lawn to work with. You also want to invest in one type of plantable that will run off the edge of the Second Life window, even if it's just one tall tree. The

Landscaping Lite

If you're not the type who wants to putter endlessly in the garden until every little detail is perfect, here are a few suggestions for reducing your time investment in landscaping:

- Use Linden plants, flowers, and trees if you can (the owner of the land decides if everybody else can have this ability), especially if you're short on cash and prims. These are freely available to everybody and are usually only 1 prim each. You can find them in the Library folder in your Inventory or planted throughout public areas built by the Lindens, such as the Help Centers.
- If you prefer (and can afford) to use plants created by residents, buy all your plantables from the same designer. Each designer uses a slightly different combination of colors, techniques, and related settings, so plantables from different "nurseries" may clash.
- Look for hand-drawn plantables, rather than ones created from photographs. The edges of a sketched or painted plant image are softer, so there's less pixilation along the transparency.
- If you don't know much about color, look for a multicolored flowering plant you like before you buy anything else. You can use additional colors from that single plant to choose everything else for your yard or garden; use only the ones you like, disregard the ones you don't, and you're all set.

FIGURE 7.13 Using one plant (hydrangea) to set a garden's color scheme.

FIGURE 7.14 Using one plant (bird of paradise) to set a garden's color scheme.

figures in the next section of this chapter, where we will fill in the hardscape with greenery, will illustrate how you can rearrange the same four or five plant-ables to achieve very different effects.

The most popular Second Life nurseries sell single plants that can't be copied, right alongside another identical plant that can be copied as much as you want. When should you pay extra for the copyable version? Do the math: How many single copies of the singleton can you get for the copyable one? Is that enough for your project? The copyable one is also best when you absolutely fall in love with a plant; when you know you want to build a "screen" with multiple copies of the same tree; or when you are planning a really large, meticulously planned garden. If none of these scenarios describes you, grab the singleton and go.

If your neighbor has a gorgeous yard or garden and you can see it, make it yours, too (see Figures 7.13–7.14). There's a time-honored tradition in real-life landscaping called *borrowed scenery*. It's the opposite of trying to design around your neighbors' choices. The idea is to invite your neighbors' landscaping in.

Plan A for borrowing scenery involves building a border wall, or rethinking your windows, to accentuate your neighbor's yard. The result? Instant beautiful view, very little work required. Plan B is to ask your gardening-obsessed neighbor if any of his/her plants are copyable, or where you can buy some for yourself. Then plant the same greenery near the border between your land and your neighbor's. Visually speaking, you just extended your neighbor's garden into your yard by using line and transition.

Landscaping Small

Don't have a yard or a garden? Maybe you live in a condo or apartment with just a tiny balcony. Maybe your sprawling Victorian mansion has a conservatory but no lawn. No worries, just read on. There are fast and easy landscaping solutions for you in Second Life, too.

- All the big garden centers in SL sell pre-potted plants and hanging flowers for the grab-and-go shopper, so feel free to grab what you like and...well...go.

- Container gardens are easy to design. Grab three pre-potted plants of varying heights instead of one. Make a triangular arrangement in a corner, with the tallest one in the back, the medium one on the left, and the shortest one on the right. Voilà, a nice tidy spot of green.

- If you only have a courtyard or patio and you'd rather invest your space and prims into nice furniture, buy some flowering vine textures for the walls. This will give you foliage and flowers without taking up any space.

Landscaping 101: Building the Hardscape

So here's what we have to work with: the little castle we built, with a stone pathway running from the street to the door and all the way around the sides. We will also be playing with a decorative stone wall to create additional definition if needed. However, we should decide right now if we want to work a focal point into the landscaping plan as a whole, and what that **focal point** should be.

Setting out the hardscape also helps to narrow down color choices for the flowers and such. A close look at the castle, the stone wall, and the pathway textures reveal that they are all a reddish sort of gray. That's why there's only a limited amount of pink in the assortment of flowering plantables chosen for this project. It's already represented.

The other color considerations have to account for the ground and the buildings on all the other lots within "sight" of this land. Take a quick panoramic glance around at all the other lots surrounding this one. The stone foundation of the castle next door and the ocean also introduce more cool colors into the scenery. Also, the multitude of greens in the grass will complement any medium or darker greens in plants.

Pale colors, however—especially something white—just wouldn't work in this scenario. Would a row of baby pink rosebushes stand out, just as an example? Yes, they definitely would. But because the other colors in the castle textures, the ground, and the other parts of the hardscape are medium to dark in tone, pale pink is too much contrast. You would have to work hard, however subconsciously, to tear your eyes away from the pink and take in any other details.

Landscaping 101: Planting the Softscape

The softscape in a landscaping project is made up from everything green and living (or, in the case of Second Life, everything green and plantable). Traditionally, also, the softscape represents the aspects of a landscape design that you can control and change with relative ease. (In the real world, you can't quickly change a brick wall, the side of a house, or most other parts of the hardscape.) So there's a yin/yang sort of relationship between the hardscape and the softscape, out of which can emerge the ultimate goal: unity.

Figures 7.15 and 7.16 show all the free plants, flowers, and trees selected for use in this landscaping project. Figure 7.15 contains all the Linden plants, which

ſLanguage

focal point *n.* Also known as a *focal*. A term borrowed from painting, architecture, photography, and many other creative endeavors. In landscaping, a focal point is a design element that serves as the "centerpiece" for all other plantings and features. Focal points can be natural, such as a flowering tree, or they can be artificial, such as a birdbath. Large gardens or yards may also have more than one focal point, if a single large focal is too expensive or otherwise prohibitive. Gardens or yards surrounding large buildings may also feature a series of small focals that lead the eye towards, or set the expectation for, a single large focal at the far rear and end of the landscaping journey.

FIGURE 7.15 Landscaping palette #1: Linden and free trees, plants, and flowers.

FIGURE 7.16 Landscaping palette #2: Resident-created trees, plants, and flowers.

⊘ **Don't Do It!**

The "Free To Copy" label on Second Life objects can be confusing, so pay attention: you only need to Select > More > Take Copy the object once. Free To Copy objects distribute copies of themselves that are also free to copy. In other words, if you see a fern you like, and you need three of them for your yard, don't grab three originals. Grab one fern only; when you're back at home and back at work, you can select-drag three copies from your Inventory. This strategy will keep your Inventory far less cluttered and all the stuff in your inventory much easier to browse.

have two distinct advantages. First, they are provided free in the Library folder of your Inventory under Objects > Landscaping > Trees, Plants, and Grasses, and second, they only "cost" one prim each. Figure 7.16, by contrast, contains all the plants designed by and purchased from other SL residents. It's no accident that most of the flowering plantables are in this grouping. Generally speaking, Linden shrubs, trees, and other all-green things are just as good as their equivalents offered for sale. But if you want really good scale, detail, and color in your flowers, it's best to spend money for them.

Note the significant difference in height—there is one or more plantable of every height category represented here. Also, notice that the colors chosen are all rich and jewel-toned, even the greens. None of these hues will get washed out against the saturated color of the ground or the somber color of the castle.

The trees and shrubs are just as substantial as the castle, too. Tall, narrow, opaque textures like the bark of these deciduous trees and the thick evergreens will help frame different parts of the garden—especially when the castle is behind the camera or otherwise out of view. Overall, the landscaping palette chosen for this project is pretty but not pastel, textured but not delicate, and otherwise entirely appropriate for the type of house at its center.

Now that you've made a plan and made some purchases, it's time to set out all the plants and start experimenting. In this section of the chapter, we're going to set out the little castle on the DYSL Resource Center land and put all this landscaping knowledge to use.

Softscape #1: Neat and Pretty

Our first design is quite simply neat and pretty (see Figures 7.17–7.18).

This look is classic, inviting, and orderly. The symmetry achieved by using multiple copies of the same plants, arranged by height from front to back, will make passersby stop and look. Visitors will feel welcome. Your neighbors will be lowering their walls and enlarging their windows to get a better view.

The neat and pretty landscape design is also the most transparent in terms of privacy. That is, there are no real obstacles created by either the hardscape or the softscape. You can see clear across the length and width of this property at a glance, from one side to the other, with just a glance. That openness conveys an attitude of friendliness and approachability, because no part of the garden is truly obscured from view.

Don't Do It!

Don't plant anything three-dimensional against the outside walls of a building. Tall trees are okay, if the leafy parts branch out well above the roofline; flat trellises or panels of ivy are also workable. Everything else will stick through the wall texture and be extremely distracting, especially if the plants are flexible and wave in the wind.

FIGURE 7.17 Looking down on two sides of the castle: the neat and pretty garden.

FIGURE 7.18 Looking down on two sides of the castle: the neat and pretty garden.

Softscape #2: The Classics

Our second design will also be popular with the neighborhood association (see Figures 7.19–7.20 on the next page).

In a word, this design is restrained. The focal point of this landscaping scheme is the castle, so the view of it is relatively uncluttered. A bit more wrought iron was added to both entrances to the property; these are arbors designed to be covered with flowers, but they work just as well as gates, too. The tall Italian-style cypress trees add a touch of texture without being too conspicuous. Color

FIGURE 7.19 Looking down on two sides of the castle: the classics garden.

FIGURE 7.20 Looking down on two sides of the castle: the classics garden.

is applied with the same idea in mind using red roses. All in all, the focal in this landscape design is the castle and its magnificent textures. Both the hardscape and the softscape accentuate rather than compete, which is what makes them successful.

A quick tweak of this garden scheme will create fairytale shabby chic. You can also create a neglected sensibility with color. If you want to play up the Sleeping Beauty mystique, go for lots and lots of rose bushes bearing blossoms in some vivid, unnatural color. Blue roses, for example, are impossible to find in real life without food coloring or scientific intervention. So they will look beautiful, yet wild and slightly wrong.

Alternatively, you can take the "Rivendell" approach—the visual color language Peter Jackson used to describe the age, grace, and decline of the elven culture in the *Lord of the Rings* movies. Situate autumn colors, brown leaves, and spindly trees against pale stone or marble. This combination of colors, textures, and materials conveys faded grandeur and waning beauty—something wistful rather than forgotten.

For our third look, let's pull out all the stops.

Softscape #3: The Dark and Stormy Night

This name is deliberately cliché, because in Second Life, you really can create an environment straight out of a kitschy pulp novel. Furthermore, you can make kitsch look just this side of tasteful *and* serve a purpose (see Figures 7.21–7.22).

FIGURE 7.21 Looking down on two sides of the castle: the "dark and stormy night."

FIGURE 7.22 Looking down on two sides of the castle: the "dark and stormy night."

Chances are pretty good nobody will want to borrow this scenery (unless you live in a community of vampires, goths, zombies, or voodoo practitioners). Regardless of the particular theme you're embracing, if you've committed to a specific sort of landscaping plan, you should play it up to the hilt. Detail matters. So let's approach this creepy version of the castle with an eye on the small stuff.

The high, dense hedge is deliberately constructed to stand just above eye level if you're beside it. From a distance, this hedge hints at any number of creepy, mysterious things on the other side—a labyrinth, a collection of headstones sticking up out of the lawn, or an elegant yet forbidding crypt. Weeping willows and dead trees complete the imposing frame for the garden, and the deep purple flowers add just a subtle hint of color. If you have the prims, the money, and the inclination, some ruined statuary would be nice as focal points. This type of addition should be the icing, though, and not the cake. If you add too many non-plant items after you've put in the softscape, you run the risk of having to start over from scratch.

Landscaping 101: The Finishing Touches

After you've planted everything the way you want, you can install the next layer of authenticity to your design with light, water, and sound. Judicious use of these elements will make your landscaping feel more authentic, as authentic as is possible in Second Life. Or, alternatively, light and sound in particular can "stage" your landscape to be extra dramatic. Let's use the "dark and stormy night" landscaping scenario to explore some examples. There are three more elements we will add to this landscaping plan, as a way of learning a few more design-related tricks.

As an example of themed design, we're going to tweak this third and final landscaping scenario to play up a vampire theme. What changes can we make to send this message? On the one hand, there's a fairly universal set of symbols that spell it all out—garlic, crosses, holy water, coffins, and so on. On the other, there are many different vampire cultures within Second Life, each embracing the world and culture of a different vampire character, film, novel, role-playing game, and so on. So when you're building a themed design such as this example, you want to be as generic as possible, so all the different "denominations" of vampires will feel welcome.

First, we will use torches and time-of-day settings to add spots of light at strategic places throughout the garden. Next, we will add a fountain of blood. Finally, we will play with the sun itself to choose the perfect time of day or

General Design Advice: Mixing Fantasy and Reality

If you're going to spend loads of time, Lindens, and effort to create an authentic themed build, everything about it should be in-theme. Don't park your Maserati in front of your Polynesian A-frame. Don't put a widescreen TV in the front parlor of your antebellum plantation house. However, if you absolutely insist on living in Hobbiton and setting out your semiautomatic weapons, you have two popular options for keeping your carefully designed environment entirely IC, or "in character."

First, put your modern life behind a period/themed door in an OOC ("out of character") room and keep it there. Create a special landmark in that room that allows you to "sneak in" from the rest of SL, so you change your clothes, titler, and so on. This strategy helps ensure that you will be in theme before you step outside.

Alternatively, you can float a skybox that is overhead—way overhead—and keep your 21st century life confined up there. If you opt for this approach, you should install a teleporter to beam yourself discreetly up and down. If you're living in a themed or role-playing area where you need a skybox, it's very likely that humans can't fly in that universe.

Why bother with all this extra work and planning? The name of this game is neighborly consideration. Residents of Second Life who gravitate toward themed areas really want to lose themselves in whatever the particular, fantastical time, place, or situation may be. So do your best *not* to interrupt someone else's fun, and they won't interrupt yours.

night that suits the color palette of our design. These three elements will transform any landscape into a truly three-dimensional Second Life experience.

➡️ **Don't Forget the DYSL Resource Center!**

For free fire, water, plants, textures, and other essential building materials, visit the DYSL Resource Center in Second Life. You can also find landmarks at the Center, which will take you to the stores/vendors that sell non-freebie stuff pictured here.

Landscaping Accents: Fire and Light

We could put modern lights out and around our little castle, if the goal were simply to provide ambiance. But we're also going for authenticity, so fire is by far the better choice. From a design standpoint, too, fire can draw attention to dark, unlit areas if it is positioned skillfully. So we are going to work with torches to further manipulate someone's experience of walking through this landscape.

Technically speaking, fire in Second Life is built like a plant and behaves like water (see Figure 7.23). Multiple copies of flat "flaming" prims are placed at 90-degree angles to each other, the same way flat pictures of plants are positioned to mimic dimensionality. As with water, you'll find that motion, sound, and ambient light are added to SL fire with scripts to complete the illusion.

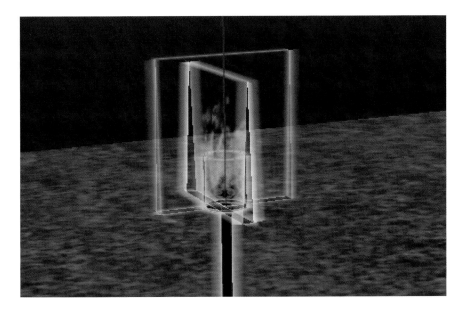

FIGURE 7.23 The building blocks of Second Life fire, highlighted with the Build > Edit tool.

The warm, golden light emitted by some Second Life fire has a limited radius, just like the real thing. For this reason, the height at which you position a fiery light source is very important. The torches used in this landscape design have been set, very carefully, to three meters (or six feet) high. The reach of this "firelight" helps obscure what is above and below them, even as it simultaneously reveals what's nearby.

In this particular landscape design, the torches serve a similar function to the stone path by creating line. The path is a literal vehicle, leading visitors away from the road and towards the castle. But the torches draw the eye to the sarcophagus at the back, and to the fountain of blood at the front corner.

Landscaping Accents: Water

Any time you add a water element to a garden, you are introducing a focal point that will dominate all others. This fountain draws on all the senses, even though it's just a virtual object, because it has color, motion, and sound. You can always count on water to provoke this type of reaction. But in terms of this landscaping design, we can use this expectation to create a surprise.

Water in Second Life is a combination of textures, prims, and oftentimes scripts. Texture gives SL water its distinctive ripply appearance. Prim-shape defines the influence of real-life gravity. Scripts make SL water behave and sound realistic. For example, in this fountain there are four prims making up the water (see Figure 7.24). There's a watery shallow cylinder in the basin for starters, to mimic the effect of the "pool." Then there are also three watery torii that create the downward cascade effect, from the top to the middle of the fountain, and the middle to the bottom.

⊘ Don't Do It!

Do *not* Unlink an object just to edit or change one part of it. It's just too easy to nudge one part out of place and mess the whole thing up.

The four objects highlighted in Figure 7.24 are the ones we want to target to make the water into blood. The Edit Linked Parts tool enables you to tweak just a few parts of a finished object without having to rebuild or rework the whole thing. First, click the object to select it (the fountain, for example), choose Edit from the Pie menu, and then click the square blue Edit icon. Check the Edit Linked Parts box, up near the top-left corner of the dialog box. Now you can click one part of the object—for example, just one watery object in this fountain—or hold down the Shift key and click more than one object to edit all of them together simultaneously.

The secret to creating blood—or any liquid other than water—is to combine a water texture with color. Unfortunately, you can't achieve authentic-looking blood, because Second Life doesn't render viscosity very well. But you can definitely tint the contents of this fountain to look startlingly red, which provides good shock value Because the stone parts of the fountain are medium bluish gray, true red was the best color for turning the water into blood. To change the color, use the Edit Linked Parts procedure spelled out previously and click the Color window to open the Pick: Color dialog box. Look for the R, G, and B value text boxes near the upper-left corner and type 255 into the R box. This will change the Current Color box into pure red. Click the Select button, close out the Edit dialog box, and the transformation is complete. The liquid contents of the fountain are now deep, bloody red (see Figure 7.25).

A final touch to any landscape design, if desired, is the manipulation of the sun. If you have ownership rights to a piece of land, you can freeze the position of the sun in the sky over that land. The four phases of the sun in Second Life are Sunrise, Noon, Sunset, and Midnight; by default, the sun will pass through all these phases in turn at the rate of four Linden days per real life day. However, if you lock in the sun at a particular phase, you can significantly affect the color, intensity, and quality of ambient light.

FIGURE 7.24 The four watery objects that make up the fountain, highlighted with the Build > Edit tool.

FIGURE 7.25 The dark and stormy night landscape with torches and the blood fountain in place.

To freeze the sun in the sky, choose Region/Estate from the World drop-down menu and click the Terrain tab (see Figure 7.26). A long, narrow picture of the sun in four phases is located, with a slider bar, near the upper-right corner of the Terrain tab page. To enable this tool, uncheck the box labeled Use Estate Sun and check the box just below it labeled Fixed Sun. Now you can adjust the position of the slider bar to any point between or among the four sun phases and click Apply when you've made a decision.

FIGURE 7.26 The World > Region/Estate > Terrain settings.

Naturally, vampires only come out at night, so we will play with the phase settings between Sunset and Sunrise. Nighttime light in Second Life is not just decreasingly bright; it is also decreasingly warm in tone. The dark and stormy night landscape design is dominated by cool and dark colors—grays, blacks, purples, blues, and deep greens (see Figure 7.27). This makes the warm fire-light of the torches, the rich hue of the roses, and the vibrant red blood in the fountain even more important as focal points. So we want to nudge the phase slider to a position where the ambient light is mostly cool with maybe just a touch of gold or crimson sun—at the very last moment of sunset, or just before the dawn.

In the next chapter, we will bring all the various individual design lessons, tips, and strategies together to build the ultimate Second Life project: a whole island. If it's your dream to create a palatial home, an in-world business center, a shopping mall, or anything grand and large in scale, Chapter 8 is definitely your next stop.

ADDITIONAL CREDITS

You can find all the brand, style, color, and designer information on items shown in the figures in the online appendix you get when registering your book at at www.peachpit.com/secondlife. See page v for details.

FIGURE 7.27 The final product: a landscaped garden that's dark, stormy, and perfectly vampire.

chapter 8

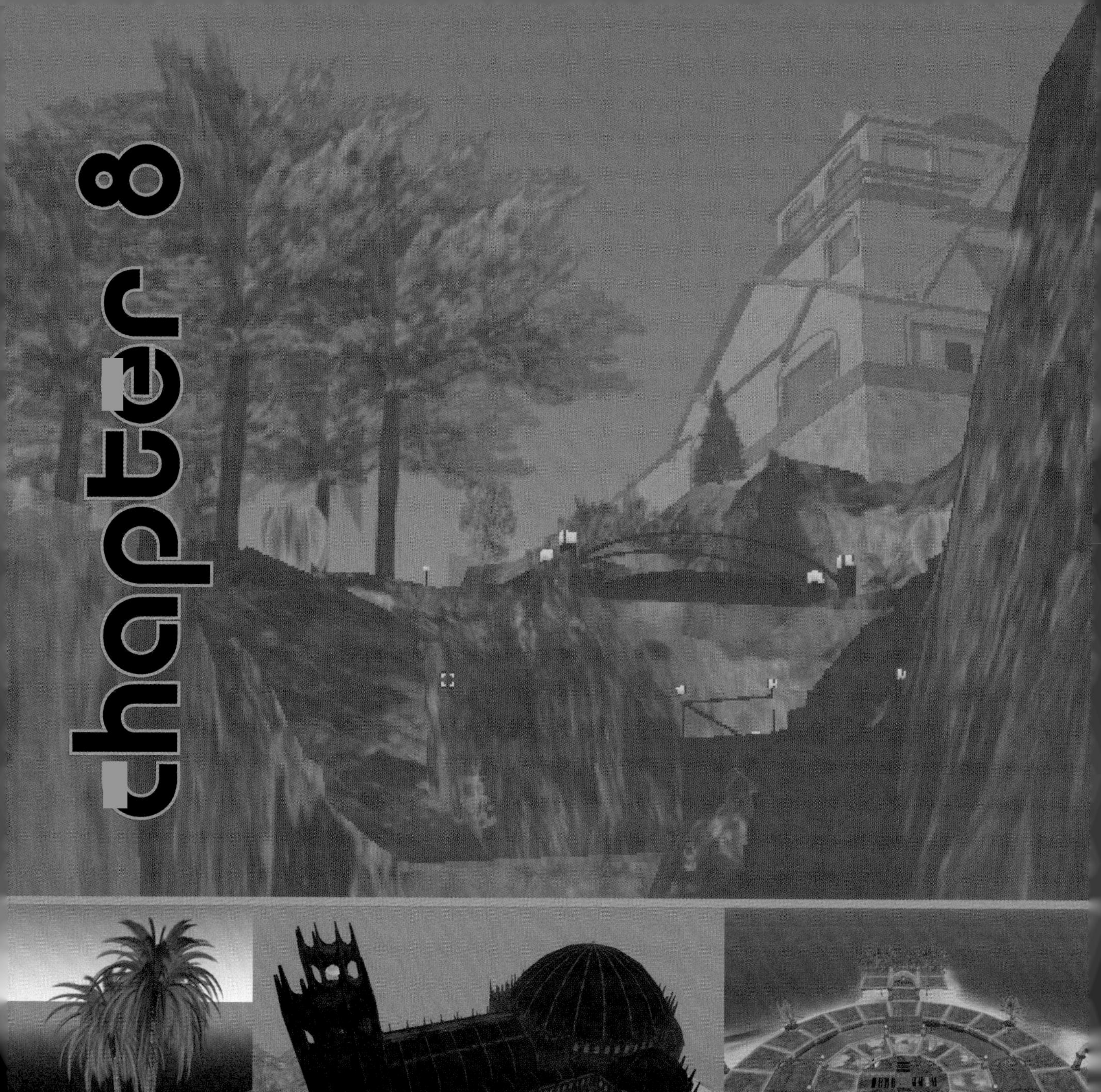

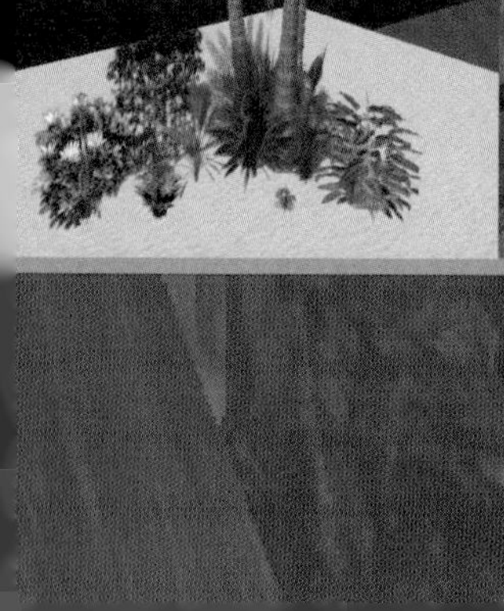

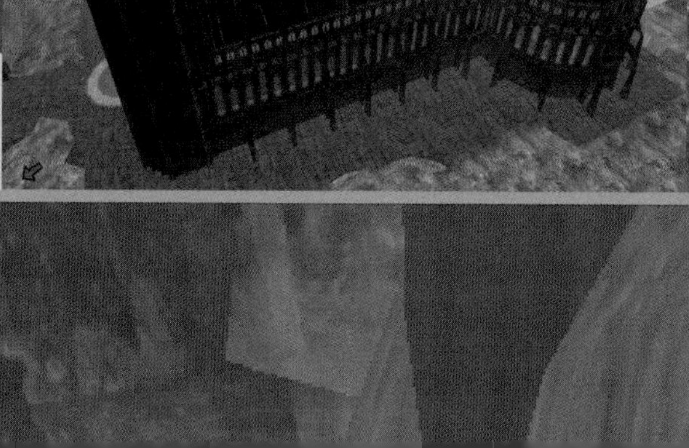

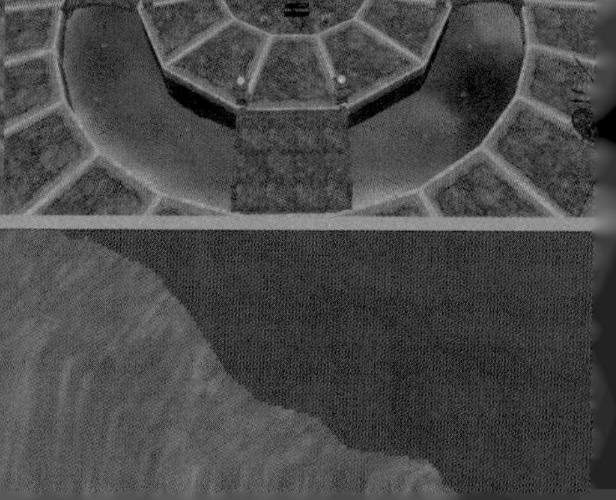

DESIGNING YOUR EMPIRE

In this chapter, you'll find the most advanced design techniques and strategies, building on the scenarios discussed in Chapters 6 and 7 (no pun intended). We'll talk about urban planning and design as it relates to Second Life and SL residents' expectations, conscious or otherwise. We'll cover large-scale landscaping and construction of a whole community with a central shared village space, not just a single house with outbuildings. We'll delve into the specialized and tricky world of building smoke, fire, and steam. We'll also explore basic terraforming—the art of customizing the actual land into mountains, islands, lakes, caves, and any other sort of topography you can imagine.

First, though, you have to have the space, the prims, and the freedom to go all out before you can turn such grand visions into virtual reality. The easiest way to secure all these resources for yourself is to buy your own private island. So let's talk about something a little more practical—creating a whole new piece of land just for you.

The Brave New World: Private Islands

Believe it or not, there comes a point when it is cheaper to buy your own property than to rent or purchase someone else's. A quick trip through the real estate Classifieds will make you raise your eyebrows in disbelief, but get out your calculator and do the math. The cumulative costs of buying a large parcel of mainland property, or renting a big parcel from another resident, are the issue. This is also the reason why very large parcels—8092 sq/m or more—are harder to find. Second Life residents have learned the hard way that smaller parcels sell, and bigger ones are best broken up.

Cheaper is relative, of course. At this writing, the fee Linden Lab charges for creating a private island is almost U.S. $2,000, and the monthly tier fee is a couple hundred U.S. dollars *in addition* to the U.S. $9.95 membership fee on a Premium account. That's a lot of money to shell out just for personal fun and games. So most residents can't afford it—unless they form a community enterprise.

For the purposes of this chapter, a community enterprise is any sort of private island development that offers something to other residents in exchange for money. You can make money in other ways on a smaller or one-time scale by getting a job, renting commercial space from another resident, even selling land you've outgrown. But the most reliable and profitable way to afford your Second Life is to own both the land and the community enterprise yourself.

Assuming you can afford it, there are other advantages to living on your own private island. You shouldn't discount these considerations just because they aren't financial.

○ **A private island is 65,536 sq/m in size, and it supports 15,000 prims.** All that space and all that raw material is all yours, unless or until you want to share, and even then you get to decide how much to keep.

○ **Private islands put far more technical control into your hands.** How much control? You never have to let another resident onto your island unless you want to. You don't even have to make your island visible to the rest of SL unless you want to. You can play your own music, choose your own terrain, set the rating, ban anybody for breaking rules you establish, and much more.

○ **You choose your neighbors—if you choose to have neighbors at all.** Your island can be all residential, all commercial, or some of each, depending solely on your wishes.

A Word or Two for Real-Life Business Owners

IF YOU HAVE A BUSINESS in real life and there's even the smallest chance you want to extend its presence into Second Life, you will want to do this on your own private island. The most compelling reason is brand identity—look at all the preceding reasons through the lens of entrepreneurial development. Now try to imagine building your ideal SL presence on the mainland, or on someone else's private island. What if a strip club or casino moves in next door? What if your landlord sells the land out from underneath you? Do you really want to leave any part of your business' success up to chance? The answer is no, of course. So postpone your in-world launch until you can afford or justify a private island; you really will be glad you did.

○ **There is far less lag on a private island than on the mainland.** That's because you control the number of active scripts, high-resolution textures, and other culprits often responsible for slowing down the grid.

How to Purchase a Private Island

To purchase a private island, visit the Second Life Land Store (shown in Figure 8.1).

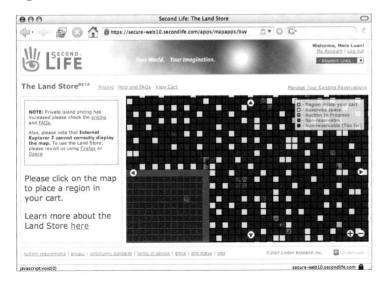

FIGURE 8.1 The Land Store: http://secure-web10.secondlife.com/apps/mapapps/buy

The first step in the ordering process is choosing a location. The big graph-paper image at the right side of the Land Store Web page is a representation of the actual Second Life grid. Your task is to find a free square on this grid that has no other claimed/occupied/reserved squares around it. This is not as easy as it sounds, and it's highly unlikely that you can choose an exact location for yourself.

It's possible to pan around with the arrow and zoom tools, click around a bit, and find out who has reserved or occupied the squares in your immediate vicinity. Occupied squares (the ones that look like real land) will tell you the names of the owner and of the island itself. Reserved squares (the yellow ones) may or may not tell you the name of the residents who placed the reservation. You can use this information in-world to Search for any listings or Profile information you can find, and this might help you figure out what kind of neighbors or neighborhoods you'll have nearby. But selecting a location on the grid is usually a free-for-all, especially as the grid gets more and more crowded.

After you do find a free square, click Add to Cart and then click Checkout. Now you'll be offered two choices: to reserve the grid space you chose, or to proceed with purchasing a private island.

Reserving Private Islands

If you're not quite ready to buy a private island, you can choose to reserve one. However, there are pros and cons:

- First and foremost, you already have to own a private island or you aren't allowed to make reservations. (Linden Lab refers to this type of member in the private island FAQ as a *concierge user.*)
- A land reservation is not a guarantee you'll get that space on the grid. When you place a reservation, you actually start an auction as the highest bidder, but there's still a possibility another resident will come along and outbid you.

- Land reservations last for three months and cost U.S. $30 per month. At the end of the three months, you can choose to extend the reservation or renew it. These fees are not applied to the fee if you end up buying an island, though.
- Land reservations don't shorten your wait time if you decide to purchase a private island; nor do they get you any other sort of preferential customer service.
- Land reservations *do* keep other residents from building within a certain distance from your existing private islands. So there's a certain logic in creating several reservations around any private island you already own, if you can afford it.

If you agree to all the terms and conditions involved in buying a private island, click Purchase. Now you can establish your region options: Region Name, Estate Name, Rating, and Region Type. Just to refresh your memory from Chapter 1, the region name is the name of this particular private island, while the estate name is the name of all the islands you own collectively. They don't have to be the same, and they don't even have to be logical. But Linden Lab does insist that both these names comply with a few restrictions:

○ Region and estate names may only be 20 characters long including spaces.

○ Region and estate names may not contain the terms *Linden*, *Second Life*, or *SL*.

○ Region and estate names may not be the same as the names of any existing private islands.

○ Region and estate names may not include special characters.

Region and estate names are also subject to review, so don't use any words you couldn't use when you named your avatar. You'll only delay the arrival of your island (and 7 to 10 days already feels like an eternity when you're itching to get to work).

There are two possible ratings for your private island: PG and M. This is more or less a no-brainer. If there is any chance something will happen on your private island that a minor should not see, choose M. Most Second Life residents are smart enough to know that an M rating doesn't guarantee that something naughty or explicit will happen, and most are courteous enough to keep that behavior away from PG areas.

Region Type is a nice effort on Linden Lab's part to save you some terraforming. The tan-colored areas on these maps are beachfront, the green areas are slightly higher, and the gray areas are mountainous. If you want to do lots of **terraforming** yourself, Region Type 3 is the flattest and easiest to work with. If you're not interested in this degree of design, choose one of the other Region Types so you can dive right into building and landscaping.

The last steps in the purchasing process are straightforward: click Next Step and confirm your account information if you like. (This gives you the chance to charge this enormous amount of money to a different funding source.) Click Proceed to Final Step and then click Submit. Now comes the wait—at least 7 to 10 business days, quite often more like 10 to 14 because private island orders are so numerous. However, you can use this time to plan your design strategy or to perfect the plan if you've already gotten started.

Large-Scale Region Development in Second Life

Designing an entire private island region "the right way" is a very detailed, time-consuming process. It's also highly individual, because every private island will ultimately serve a unique purpose, even if it's one of dozens, hundreds, or thousands owned by the same person. However, there are a few design-related considerations that will always hold true, no matter what you end up doing with your private island. These basic concepts are centered on urban planning, usability design, and other practices that take visitors, customers, or travelers into account.

Urban planning and design address the task of growing communities wisely and responsibly. In real life, this challenge considers everything from public transportation and environmental concerns to economic growth and civil engineering. In Second Life, the focus is tighter, and the overall concern is largely financial—whether or not you can afford to keep your private island property by making it pay for itself. However, your chances for success can be greatly increased by adopting many of the strategies involved in real-life urban planning. People have certain expectations about what makes a private island inviting, functional, and impressive, and these expectations have been formed in part by their real-life experiences out in real-life towns and cities.

Many of these real-life aspects of urban planning and design carry over into Second Life:

- **Structure:** The way that all buildings relate to one another, both visually and functionally.
- **Accessibility:** The ease, safety, and freedom with which residents can (or cannot) move from point to point.
- **Wayfinding**: The ease with which residents can (or cannot) find their way around, both with and without assistance.
- **Animation**: Whether or not an area encourages residents to participate in some sort of activity, on their own or in a group.
- **Function and fit:** The act of designing a building, general location, or area to support and encourage a particular use.

- **Order and incident**: Whether or not a building, general location, or area allows for spontaneous or predictable activity, with the goal of encouraging both

- **Consistency and variety:** The frequency with which a building, general location, or area produces the type of activity for which it was designed

If all these terms seem too overwhelming individually, think of them in terms of an example community enterprise: a racetrack. Let's say you buy a private island and build yourself an authentic Kentucky horse ranch. You research the design meticulously and create a grand, plantation-style mansion, green rolling hills, and a dirt oval-shaped track for your very own Derby.

Your idea is simple: invite residents to race horses for an entry fee, and take bets as a bookie. You build stands and a barn; you plant all the right flowers and trees to simulate a mild, Appalachian climate; and finally you advertise your Grand Opening day in Search. In the interim, you get plenty of foot traffic as people come through to look around. Some people test the track with their horses. About half a dozen residents say they'll race. But on the big day itself, the turnout is disappointing. What happened?

The most productive way to troubleshoot your own community enterprise is to teleport off your private island, use Search to locate it, and then TP back in just as any random visitor would. Pretend you've never been to your island before. Is the very first thing you see what you expected? Is there something at the entry point to suggest where you can or should go next—a sign, a path, a road? Can you see anything interesting or beautiful that draws you toward it? Is that interesting or beautiful thing associated with the purpose of your community enterprise?

Of course, technical issues can (and do) tank a wonderful idea in a heartbeat. So in the case of your racetrack, recruit a few of your friends to run a race with you. Do all the horses run smoothly and swiftly, or limp along, or both? How many horses can run together without causing enthusiasm-killing lag? If you have scripted features to your track, like a finish line or a betting kiosk, check and check again to make sure that they are functioning properly. Most importantly, if you find something that doesn't work like you assumed it would, don't kick yourself, just fix it. Second Life is a remarkably resilient as a technical environment *and* as a community. People may very well come back and hang in there with you, if you can deliver what you promise eventually.

This Space Available: Commercial, Residential and Public Space

In Second Life, if you're building anything other than your own home, you're building one of three types of spaces—commercial, residential, or public. Commercial space is just what it sounds like: where business or commerce of some sort will take place. Residential space is where other people will live, either in buildings you provide or in homes they construct. Public space is transitional, usually set aside for scenery or travel between other locations. The large-scale design challenges for each zone type are distinctly different, yet equally important, and there are a few tasks all these design processes have in common.

Preparation for Large-Scale Design

Everybody building on a grand scale in Second Life has a different modus operandi. Sometimes it's fun and exciting to work on the fly and just see what inspiration strikes while you're messing with the SL tools. Other builders and designers enjoy the R&D: making drawings, charts, and other plans before they set down a single prim. In this section of the book, you'll walk through a middle-of-the-road approach. These three phases—measuring space, brainstorming designs, and approximating layout—involve nearly equal amounts of spontaneity and organization. So this is a good place for you to start, no matter where you happen to fall on the preparation spectrum.

Prep Step #1: Measuring Space

First, decide how much square meterage you want to dedicate to any other purpose than your own. This might sound like another no-brainer, especially if you've already finished building your house and such. However, this is where the relationship between prims and square meterage really comes into play. You don't want to use up every last prim, or give up the use of those last few prims to someone else.

Now is the time to think long and hard about any future needs for prims you might have. Then add a number to that total that's between 350 to 500. These two numbers are your buffers. You'll have your own personal prim reserve, to indulge yourself later on if you want. Your private island will also have its own reserve (prims that will never be used) to guard against the technical issues that occur if a region approaches maximum usage.

However, you can't truly control a prim reserve without also controlling an equivalent amount of land. Many residents who own private islands never consciously consider this. They just build what they want for themselves, divvy up the rest of their property for various moneymaking purposes, and concentrate on how much rent they can earn. Then the day comes (and inevitably, it does) when the owner has "sold" too many prims, and there aren't enough to keep the island from maxing out. What's the solution—evict a tenant or two? Or sacrifice prims of your own? If you're really money-minded, and you have even an iota of common sense, the choice is obvious. You have to give up part of your own freedom to play.

So it's time to measure your land, and measure it accurately. The easiest way to do this is to fly overhead, use the Camera Controls to look down, and open the Build tools. Click the right-most blue icon at the top of the dialog box: Land. The Land-related tools will appear (see Figure 8.2).

FIGURE 8.2 The Land tab page in the Build tools dialog box.

All the land underneath you will turn pale blue. Click once on the ground, anywhere there is open land, and a transparent yellow square will appear. This square highlights one 16 sq/m of piece of the private island, even if it's sunken land covered in water. By clicking and dragging in this mode, you can expand the square and select a very large area. Now click the More button on the right side of the Land tab page, and the page will extend. There will be a measurement in sq/m, marked as "Area," on the left. This is the measurement of all the land inside that outline you drew on the ground (see Figure 8.3).

FIGURE 8.3 Selecting land with the Build > Land > Select Land tool.

Next, calculate the number of prims you have to work with—to refresh your memory on the formula, it's the size of the land in square meters multiplied by 15,000 and then divided by 65,536. For the sake of argument, let's say your homestead measures 4,096 square meters. This gives you a personal "allowance" of 937 prims. 937 is also pretty close to the number you had in mind for your overall prim reserve, which means 4,096 sq/m of land needs to remain permanently unused. (We'll talk about various strategies for this land later in the chapter.) The grand total is 8,192 sq/m, and 1,874 prims that you cannot use to make a profit.

Prep Step #2: Brainstorming Designs
If you've already built your own house/garden on your private island, you've given yourself a place to start with designing the rest of your property. Walk out the front door or front gate and turn around about 20 meters or so. Look

back on what you've already built; what does the front of your property look like? Use the infrastructure of what you've already done—from pathways and sidewalks, to fencing or walls, to landscaping choices—as a starting point for the rest of what you want to construct.

General Design Advice: Styles Gone Wild

If your house is straight out of Georgian England and you want your commercial space to look like downtown Tokyo, there are two possible strategies you can use to make this work. You can do some serious transition with walls and public space. Or you can put your Jane Austen-ish homestead on a big platform and float it as a skybox, leaving all the land free and clear for creating a modern neon jungle.

You should also spend time thinking about what you want to do with the rest of your private island. Do you want to rent it out as residential property and have a smaller number of Second Life residents hanging out as neighbors? Or do you want to build some sort of shopping complex, or office space, or event destinations like a club, and have lots of SL residents coming and going?

Finally, no matter how much development you decide to do, you can't forget to put in sufficient public space. Even though every resident can fly, most private islands still have some sort of path or road system, especially if every part of it is designed for interactive use. It's also good design to create a nicely proportioned space around the entry point; this creates a good first impression. You yourself will want a minimum of 20 meters as a "cushion" between the edge of your homestead and the edge of whatever else you build. This guarantees you audible privacy and draws a psychological boundary most residents will know not to cross.

Prep Step #3: Approximating Layout

Now, it's time to get down to specifics: How many discrete areas of commercial, residential, or public space are you going to build? How will these different types of spaces be arranged? If it helps to clear your head, get out pencil and paper, or open a graphics program and draw yourself a preliminary patchwork grid. When you're reasonably satisfied with your plan, open the Camera Controls and the Build tools, and use the Land tool options to **parcel** your land.

Parceling is not necessary, but in the long run it's generally a good idea if only to control the use and distribution of prims. Before or unless you parcel, the Second Life grid won't keep track of how and where your 15,000 prims are being used. If you're on your private island all alone, this isn't necessarily a problem. But imagine it's you plus lots of tenants, each building busily away, and nobody is keeping a close eye on their individual prim allowances. There's nothing to stop one resident from using up more than his or her share, other than a general sense of fairness and goodwill.

On the other hand, if it's you and your tenants sharing a private island, and everybody's land is parceled, the grid is now "turned on." Someone can try to put more than 937 prims on a 4,096 sq/m parcel, but they'll fail *and* they'll get the Second Life equivalent of an error message. Plus, most importantly, nobody else on the private island is affected. The rest of you can go on with your work with confidence.

Parceling has two immediate advantages. First, nothing is blocking your view of the land while you use the Build > Land > Select Land tool. It's considerably more difficult to go back and parcel property after it's been covered with buildings, plants, and so on. Second, parceling before you build will tell you exactly how many prims will be left over for a tenant. This will keep your designs under restraint in terms of both size and complexity. No matter how beautiful or unique the space you offer might be, if there are insufficient prims left over for a tenant to use, nobody will rent it.

Now let's zero in on the three types of space: commercial, residential, and public.

Large-Scale Design: Commercial Space

There's a lot of commercial space in Second Life—a lot—and frankly, the majority of it is a mess. This is the reason why many designers build their own stores; most commercial landlords simply build something that looks cool or different. Commercial space must be functional, first and foremost, and its function is far more complicated than many residents really think.

From single stores to sprawling malls, the goal of commercial space is the same, and so is the symbiotic relationship between all the key players:

○ Owners of the land underneath commercial space seek to pay their bills by subletting to tenants, without giving up too many prims or too much square meterage.

○ Tenants take on a rental agreement as a calculated risk, betting on both the storefront and their own goods or services to attract customers.

○ Customers want a comfortable problem-free shopping experience, which largely depends on how the owner designs and maintains the commercial space.

All of that probably sounds patently obvious, and it *is* a circular dilemma. But you'd be surprised how much room there is in this equation for misunderstanding and selfishness, which leads inevitably to failure. So if you're the owner in this scenario, how can you rise to this challenge both wisely and efficiently? Step by careful step.

Look at these examples of commercial property (see Figures 8.4–8.6).

General Design Tip: Retail Space

If you're designing retail space, you should think about how to accommodate all three of these types of vendors, or whether or not you want to restrict the type of vendors that tenants can use. However, do not decide to forbid a certain type of vendor because the way it looks or works will look out of place on your private island. Even in the most rigorous role-playing regions, and in the stores that cater to those role-players, everybody in Second Life accepts that modern-looking scripted vendors are a necessity.

FIGURE 8.4 The Heart to Heart Garden Center, one of the largest Second Life "greenhouses."

FIGURE 8.5 Panache, a light and airy hair salon.

FIGURE 8.6 Textures R Us, a very popular textures supplier.

Heart to Heart took the logical approach to selling its trees and flowers in situ, spread out like an actual garden. But the arrangement of goods for sale is so lovely, customers don't mind having to roam around. Panache offers one of the widest array of color choices in women's hair, but their shelving system makes selection a snap. Textures R Us does well because their selection and quality are superior, but the main store is also spacious and easy to navigate without actually feeling immense. These three examples also show the three most common types of *vendors*, or methods by which items are traded to residents for money:

○ **The copyable original**: A copy of the actual item for sale, which sits out on display, such as a couch or a plane. The customer right- or Apple-clicks on this original to open the Pie menu, and chooses Pay to make a purchase. A copy of the item is deposited into the customer's Inventory. On the plus side, copyable originals rarely contribute to lag like other vendor types, but they eat up a lot of prims (and most commercial spaces don't give merchants a large prim allowance).

○ **The single-item vendor**: A flat single prim that usually sits or hangs upright, is textured with a picture of the item it dispenses, and hands out this item after a customer clicks-and-pays it. The advantages to this method are in saving prims; the potential disadvantages become apparent if a merchant has many items to sell (which is why many stores look wallpapered with infinite single images, stretching way over your avatar's head).

○ **The multi-item vendor**: A device that vaguely resembles a home theater system, with one main screen in the middle and sometimes multiple smaller screens running vertically along the sides, and two arrows pointing in opposite directions. These vendors can hold, display, and dispense many items for sale in a small space. The main advantage is in the prim-to-merchandise ratio, which far exceeds either of the other vendor types. However, multi-item vendors are notoriously user-unfriendly and large numbers of them in a single region will cause lag.

Design considerations for office, meeting, or classroom space are variations on the themes we addressed in Chapters 6 and 7 about room size and such. Despite the fact that you don't need to sit or be comfortable in a virtual meeting, you should still furnish Second Life corporate or educational space like its real-world counterparts. Don't make residents stand around, if only because seating arrangements keep everybody within chat range of each other (within 20 meters, just as another reminder).

FIGURE 8.7 Ansoku Studio Apartments—Japanese simplicity inside and out.

Large-Scale Design: Residential Space

Residential space design is also a redux of the same strategies and concerns you considered when building your own house. In fact, potential tenants will be pleasantly surprised if you build apartments, condos, and townhouses as if you were going to live in them yourself. A great deal of the rental property available in Second Life is plain and simple in the bad sense, which is the kiss of death, no matter how attractive you make the rent or prim allowance.

Let's look at some nicely, thoughtfully constructed residential spaces (Figures 8.7–8.9).

The Ansoku apartments provide privacy stylishly without making tenants feel isolated from each other. The Zuni Lux Apartments offer residents a gorgeous ocean view through clickable privacy windows, making privacy a choice. Aly's Homes are tucked into the side of a high green hill, creating the feeling of peace and quiet, which is sometimes all tenants want.

FIGURE 8.8 Zuni Lux Apartments—modern and spacious.

FIGURE 8.9 Aly's Homes— cute and homey country cottages.

Here are some simple ways to make rental properties attractive:

○ **Rent all prebuilt space by the week, not the month.** Second Life residents will often rent a small place to live while they are building their own homestead, waiting for their own private island to arrive, or waiting for rentable land to open up. So it is almost a cultural expectation that the rent for apartments will be payable by the week and not the month. Rentable land for building, on the other hand, is just the opposite. People attracted to that situation intend to put down roots and stay, so charging them a month at a time is just fine.

○ **Extend your design theme indoors.** Don't "paint" the interior walls of your apartments or townhouses eggshell white. If the outsides of your residential buildings are beautifully textured to complement your overall design scheme, would-be tenants expect to find that same look on the inside. You might not think this is true if your private island is themed, especially themed to a fabulous, meticulous degree. But it is.

○ **Offer visual privacy.** Invest in a texture set with at least one window option if your design calls for solid walls. Texture the inside of your apartment/townhouse walls with the "open" or transparent windows, and the outside with a shuttered or curtained window, or even a solid wall. Your tenants will be able to look out, but passersby won't be able to look in. This feature is surprisingly hard to find, so if you use it, you'll make yourself look more thoughtful, unlike many other SL landlords.

○ **Make it easy to pay rent.** Yes, it's inconvenient to cash out Lindens for real money, especially in this day and age of PayPal. But the majority of potential tenants are going to want to pay you anonymously with Lindens, even if their rent is four or five figures. To wit, make friends with the **rentalbot** of your choice. Don't put yourself or your tenants in the uncomfortable position of having to chase somebody down to pay rent.

Large-Scale Design: Public Space

Public space design is surprisingly challenging and not often taken seriously. For one thing, creating public space is the easiest way to create prim reserves, because public space doesn't need to have a lot of "stuff" in it to look authentic or correct. In most cases, all you really need is a path of some sort to suggest there's something interesting "down the road," flanked by the occasional tree, bench, fountain, or streetlight. If you think it through, that strategy doesn't take many prims, either—not when you think about the total square meterage a truly useful road will require.

However, many residents seem to underestimate the impact, usefulness, and need for public space. This is especially true in situations when the owner of a private island is driven to make as much profit as possible. Any space that can't be rented is wasted, right? Wrong.

Over and over in this book, either directly or indirectly, we've examined how people are seeing the Second Life environment—the lack of true peripheral vision, the position of the camera being above and behind your avatar's head. We've been designing interiors to allow for this enlarged "body bubble," and implied that the need extends into both the hardscape and softscape of a

SLanguage

rentalbot *n.* An object that's scripted to babysit your tenants and rental spaces so you don't have to. Rentalbots are often expensive but copyable, and always truly worth whatever you have to spend. The most common rentalbots will accept rent payments; remind tenants when rent is due and how many prims they have; offer information on rental space that's vacant; and send both you and your tenants email notifications when leases begin and expire. Some will also lock out delinquent tenants and even return their things if they don't pay. Also known as a *bot* (and a real timesaver).

good landscaping plan. Ultimately, the purpose of public space is no different. Without well-designed public space, a region feels claustrophobic, crowded, and strikingly artificial. In fact, a routine sampling of Popular Places bore this theory out—every beach, garden, grotto, or other outdoor region listed in this part of Search made intelligent use of public space.

Below are three examples of public spaces that look good and function well (Figures 8.10–8.12).

FIGURE 8.10 The Isle of Wyrms Cathedral—elegant, authentic, majestic.

FIGURE 8.11 The Shops @ Son Village—nice and simple but very effective.

FIGURE 8.12 The Dreamland Central Hub—Anshe Chung's 3D Introductory brochure.

The Isle of Wyrms is famous throughout Second Life for exquisite, elaborate dragon avatars. So it's no surprise that a cathedral makes for good gathering space; elbow room takes on a whole new meaning if your wings are several meters across. The Shops @ Son Village are, by constrast, simply suburban-American-ordinary and that's just fine. The road is the right width to be useful as both driving space for cars and as boundaries between commercial lots. The Dreamland Central Hub is also a pleasant, usable, beautiful surprise—at first glance, would you think this was Anshe Chung's official entryway/introduction to her expansive, million-dollar real estate empire? Not at all. It's comfortable in size and scale; the landmark and notecard dispensers are not obtrusive; and all the information available here is neatly and logically organized.

What considerations play a part in a well-designed public space? Think about these things:

○ **The entry point**: Remember, this is the spot where everyone will arrive if they've used Search to find your private island. It needs to be large enough to accommodate the camera and multiple visitors arriving at the same time, and it should be obviously free and clear of obstructions. If you put walls, signs, or any other tall elements too close to the entry point, it will get between a resident and his or her camera. You'll lose your only chance to make a good first impression.

○ **Information exchange**: For the sake of argument, let's say you're building space for AA or other groups dedicated to addiction management. It might be most user-friendly to put information kiosks, the kind that dispense notecards when they are right- or Apple-clicked, somewhere outside. This gives self-conscious or hesitant would-be attendees the chance to do some reconnaissance without having to walk into the actual meeting space and "be found out." The same basic premise applies to role-playing areas, too. In those scenarios, you always want to give visitors the space and opportunity to learn the rules without being yanked into the ongoing action. Give them a little area where they can wander around, read the rules on notecards, and even watch what's happening in "safety," as visitors who are having a look-see.

○ **Required elements**: Any type of build that's historical or thematic, i.e., attempting to replicate and evoke a particular time, place, location, or fictional world, needs to look the part. Furthermore, everything in the public space on your themed private island needs to both establish and prolong the fantasy. Would a Wild West gold rush town look authentic without a saloon? Probably not. Would visitors to this town know where to hang out and meet others if there was no saloon offering drinks, poker, and the chance to gossip? Again, not likely.

The best way to see all these thoughts and ideas in action is to study a living, working example of large-scale design. It wasn't feasible to create an example of this size or scale just for this book, and such a creation would lack information based on traffic, use, and interaction with the SL public. So the rest of this chapter will refer specifically to the initial plans, ongoing maintenance, and long-term development of a RP microcontinent called *Ketora*.

Read the Blog!

Visit the blog for this book at http://designingyoursecondlife.blogspot. com. It provides in-depth interviews with designers featured here in the book (such as Eonne Junot, the owner of Ketora), and even more advice from personal stylists, volunteer mentors, role-play moderators, and other residents helping to craft Second Life into the best virtual experience possible.

Large-Scale Design: The Microcontinent of Ketora

Ketora was conceived to be a dual-purpose enterprise: both a role-playing environment *and* commercial real estate. Because of this goal, certain guidelines and expectations were already in place before any plans were written down:

○ Ketora, and the next three to five private islands to be added on, would pay for themselves through residential rental income.

○ Ketora would be a Gorean role-playing environment, created and presented as a Gorean community, as defined by descriptions in John Norman's Gorean novels and certain "universal customs" imported into *Second Life* by Gorean IRC role-players.

○ Lot sizes would have to vary in size in order to attract as many possible types of Gorean "Households," from very large to very small.

○ As a Second Life Gorean community, Ketora needed to have a "home stone" or political-bureaucratic hub—namely a village, town, or city.

○ Ketora's hub needed between five and seven essential types of public buildings to appear authentic to SL Gorean role-players.

With these considerations in mind, preparation began.

Prep Step #1: Measuring Space

The initial plan for Ketora (the name by which the whole microcontinent is known) was to grow one island into three as soon as possible. So measurement-related considerations for each of the three initial islands included the following:

○ Light terraforming on all interior-side shorelines to make each island look distinct and separated by channels with sandbars

○ Space on Ketora for the village/town center

○ Space on Ketora West and Ketora East for pathways, allowing "gated" access to every rentable lot

In both John Norman's fantasy novels, and elsewhere in Second Life and online Gor, Gorean civilization is not modern. Technologically and culturally, it remains roughly equivalent to late medieval Eastern Europe. So the most common method of long-distance transportation in SL Gor is the wooden sailing ship. In fact, the entry point into the majority of SL Gorean SIMs is traditionally on the deck of a ship.

This RP requirement meant the village would have to be located somewhere on the shore (see Figure 8.13). With all options available, the ship/village/main public space was constructed along the western shore to take advantage of Second Life's amazing sunsets. The downside was financial: about one fifth of Ketora's valuable beachfront property was not available for rent.

Prep Step #2: Brainstorming Design

With the Internet, it doesn't take long to assemble a "design palette" or quilt-like collection of images, colors, textures, building materials, and other pieces-parts to stimulate the imagination. Here are a few excerpts from the design palette for Ketora: images of real storefronts and houses in San Juan, Puerto Rico; old Havana in Cuba; the French Quarter in New Orleans, Louisiana; and Caracas, Venezuela (Figure 8.14).

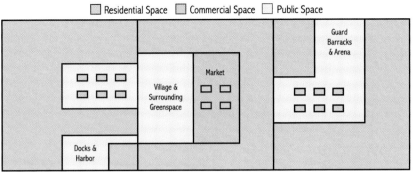

Residential Space ☐ Commercial Space ☐ Public Space

FIGURE 8.13 Measurements for the first three islands: from left to right, Ketora West, Ketora, and Ketora East.

Copyright Rafael Martin-Gaitero

Copyright ShutterVision

Copyright Chuck Aghoian

Copyright Alexandar Iotzov

FIGURE 8.14 Real storefronts and housefronts in historic San Juan, Havana, New Orleans, and Caracas.

Everything you can see in Figure 8.14 suggests the parameters for building every part of a tropical village:

○ Saturated candy/sherbet colors: peach, mint green, lemon yellow, sky blue, etc.

○ Distressed textures, such as peeling white paint and weathered stucco

○ Wrought iron banisters, fencing, gates, and railings

○ Half-pipe Spanish tile roofing in equally saturated colors, especially reds and oranges

○ Sidewalks, foundations, and steps with sand and small plants in the corners

○ Plentiful lush foliage and flowers including vines

These specifications translate into Second Life materials in the form of textures and plantables (Figures 8.15 and 8.16).

Quantity is key, in different ways, to both groups of these design elements. In Chapter 7, "Designing Your Homestead," the little castle built with rounded prims was constructed with just one texture set. Similarly, each of the textures pictured in Figure 8.15 are one in a set of anywhere from six to 20 coordinating elements. Remember that texture sets often contain everything you'd need, from garden borders and grillework to architectural trim, in addition to walls, windows, and roof textures. This versatility makes economic sense if you're

FIGURE 8.15 Example textures used to build Ketora's public spaces.

FIGURE 8.16 The trees, flowers, leafy plants, and other landscaping basics used throughout the microcontinent of Ketora.

designing a whole community. You can easily use just two or three textures to build a prominent or important public building—such as the administrative building in Ketora's village. Then you can utilize the remaining textures in the same set in subtler ways throughout other constructions in the village. This ties one large area of different buildings together visually.

All the plantables pictured in Figure 8.16 are either free to copy or for sale by their creator in bulk as "landscaping sets." They are also used on all three of the main islands—Ketora, Ketora West, and Ketora East—to tie them together for visual appeal and a touch of realism. This technique reflects the use of line on a grand scale, to bring back a concept introduced in Chapter 7. Despite the channels dividing each island from another, using the same plantables on either side implies visually that the islands are still connected.

Prep Step #3: Approximating Layout

With the arrival of the middle island, Ketora proper, most of the layout work went into designing the community hub, whether it would be a city, a town, or just a village. Proper layout in this area, along with careful composition, were crucial for a couple reasons.

First, the hub would provide the first impression to all visitors when they arrived "on the boat" in the harbor. Second, the type and position of each individual building needed to confirm an authentic "Gorean-ness." The tropical climate of Ketora diverges quite drastically from the medieval European castle look of other Gorean SIMs. Third, the ratio of public space to rentable residential space proved to be tight financially. For all these reasons, and to keep in theme with the outpost, edge-of-the-world, colonial island scenario, Ketora was constructed as a village.

For RP reasons, a Gorean community hub needs to include certain role-playing resources. However, not every place needs to have its own building. A scribery and an infirmary, for example, are common to every Gorean SIM, but they are not as frequently needed or visited as the tavern or the guardhouse. The few extras in this village design, such as the blue tent, are both beautiful and practical. The transparency of the tent silks leads the eye out across the channel, and the open design implies its function as a place for both genders to relax (which is not often provided elsewhere on SL Gor). This overall balance of eye appeal, RP value, and efficiency makes the village of Ketora unique within SL Gor.

The village as a whole also served a dual purpose while Ketora remained three islands in size. The village buildings were arranged in a semicircle facing the western channel to create a boundary for the plaza—the open area of sand labeled as such in Figure 8.17. This design created accessibility, wayfinding, function, and fit—but it also established a specific type of animation. The plaza was designed to double as an open-air arena, for medieval-style combat that all Gorean regions in SL need to guarantee foot traffic. It also keeps melee RP far away from residential tenants who want peace and quiet.

FIGURE 8.17 The village and the plaza on Ketora.

Hands-on Preparation: Terraforming

Terraforming is the first actual work you should undertake on your private island: sculpting the surface of the land before you build anything on it. To paraphrase the very popular line from *The Matrix*, though, unfortunately no one can be told what terraforming is. The only way to really learn it is to buy your own land (or find the rare public sandbox where you can practice) and have at it. However, there is some hard-earned (yet minimal) advice that does relay well in print. The main thing to know is that terraforming is notoriously difficult and results vary drastically until you figure out what you're doing.

To get started, stand nearby—repeat, nearby and *not* on—the spot you want to terraform and right- or Apple-click the bare ground. Choose Edit Terrain from the Pie menu, and the land under your feet will turn blue. Also, the Build dialog box will appear with the Land page in view and the Select Land radio button will be ticked by default.

Here's where things can get confusing. If you click the land right now, the yellow box-shaped outline appears (just as it does during parceling). You just selected that 16 sq/m area of land to terraform—more or less. This is the first thing to realize about the terraforming tools: even though the controls suggest you can edit the terrain precisely, you really can't.

To use any another tool, click another radio button—Flatten Land, Raise Land, Lower Land, Smooth Land, or Roughen Land. Now we're into *taskus interruptus*, because the cursor changed. It's now a tiny bulldozer hovering over a mesh of white dots. This is the other way to apply changes to the land—by means of this mesh. However, here's the next confusing thing: *You are still working with the land inside and just around the yellow box*. You have to ignore what the cursor is doing for now, even though it has changed appearance. Don't click on the land again—only on the Build > Land tools—or you'll get results you didn't expect.

Here are the effects of each tool, aside from how they are labeled:

○ **Flatten Land**: Creates an area of land that is perfectly level with the grid, some of which is just outside the yellow box. Creates drastic differences in height at the edges of this area, which might defeat the purpose of using the tool in the first place.

○ **Raise Land**: Raises an area of land roughly 1.5 to 2 meters high. Creates differences in height at the edges of the area, possibly defeating the purpose.

○ **Lower Land**: Lowers an area of land roughly 1.5 to 2 meters down. Creates a hole, possibly defeating the purpose.

○ **Smooth Land**: Evens out the surface of an area of land *by raising it*, which may result in making concurrent areas look distinctly unsmooth.

○ **Roughen Land**: Disturbs the surface of an area of land *by lowering it*, which may result in making concurrent areas look distinctly, unattractively different.

After you've clicked one of the radio buttons next to these options, click the Apply to Selection button and the changes will take place.

There are two main benefits to using the yellow box for terraforming. First, you can select huge tracts of land with it and be quite precise on a certain scale. Also, the Revert Land option will undo the last thing you did. (The only trick with this godsend is its limitations: You can only go one step back. So don't use a tool again, or switch and use another tool, or close the Build tool dialog box until you are absolutely satisfied.)

The primary downsides to the yellow box method are the unnatural results you get and the trap it can create as you try to fix them. The general shape of each of these terraforming effects will look square because you were using a square to achieve them, and there's no alternative. So this tool is best for large-scale adjustments to sea level, or for obviously artificial land development, like terracing or digging trenches.

Now, back to that bulldozer and the strange white mesh. This terraforming option is probably intended as a Step 2 after you use the yellow box. The mesh tweaks the harshness left behind by using the yellow box method; the mesh is a free-floating, click-and-drag type control that applies somewhat similar results to the ones mentioned previously. The key word in there is *somewhat*.

On the plus side, you can set the size of the mesh to Small, Medium, or Large; use the drop-down menu on the right side of the Build > Land dialog box. You can also sculpt the land more easily in smaller or larger sections than by selecting with the yellow box. On the negative side, the results you get with the mesh are even less precise *and* the Revert Land option doesn't work with it.

With terraforming in mind, making Ketora a tropical island was a fortuitous choice. Why? Several reasons. Such islands are commonly very flat and very close to sea level. So the most authentic look for Ketora turned out to be the easiest to accomplish. Each island was yellow-boxed into an entirely flat, perfect square, and then white-meshed along the edges to create the beach, channels, coves, and sandbars. All this empty space provided the perfect place to stash the islands' prim reserves as well; the only objects placed in these areas are bridges and the occasional rolling "wave" for visual and audio sound effects. Furthermore, creating a realistic coastline did not require perfect terraforming skills. For all these reasons, the shoreline is anything but wasted (see Figure 8.18).

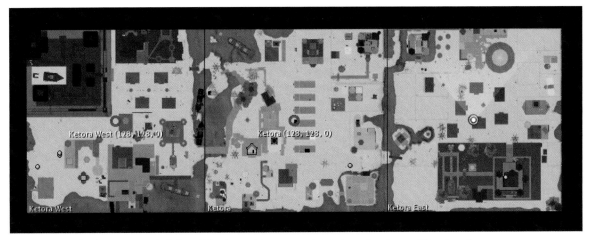

FIGURE 8.18 A bird's-eye view of all three islands, and the appropriately irregular shape of the shoreline.

Commercial, Residential, and Public Space on Ketora

Because Ketora is a role-playing environment, it is subject to RP rules that function optimally in a village-type scenario. As a result, commercial, residential, and public spaces on Ketora are especially entwined. This close proximity of such differently used space has contributed to a few specific challenges, although these challenges are far from unique to SL Gor.

Commercial Space Management and Design on Ketora

Another "required" feature of Second Life Gorean SIMs is a marketplace, some sort of open-air commercial area divided into stalls where Gorean-appropriate goods are for sale (see Figure 8.19 on the next page). However, there was no way to work a marketplace into the plan until Ketora West and Ketora East were added on. The rent from residential space on these outer islands helps offset the unpredictability of marketplace income.

On average, most malls and markets throughout Second Life (not just in role-playing areas like SL Gor) operate at 60–65% occupancy. The reasons for this seem twofold. First, as already mentioned earlier in this chapter, the majority of SL commercial space is not designed with the needs of merchants and their customers in mind. This leads into the second reason, which was also already touched upon: Whenever possible, SL merchants will buy their own private

FIGURE 8.19 The marketplace on Ketora.

islands, build their own stores, and stop renting commercial space from other residents. The eventual result is that the most successful merchants may not sell through malls and markets.

On the other hand, many merchants look at market-type commercial space as an advertising expense. If the market's location has good foot traffic or word-of-mouth recognition, then a market stall in that SIM can drive customers to the merchant's main store. That makes the expense of maintaining a market-place presence more bearable and logical. The burden for persuading merchants to embrace this approach is squarely on the owners of commercial space. Even in role-playing or highly themed areas like SL Gor, where authenticity demands as little technology as possible, an owner can offer two "perks" without break-ing the rules: provide landmark dispensers with every stall, and mention a merchant by name in the marketplace's Search listing.

Residential Space Management and Design on Ketora

For residents living on the main, center island on Ketora, the marketplace is often just steps away from their gates or front doors. For some, this is a benefit—they are closer to the bustle and hum of village life, and they can walk easily to the middle of town. For other residents, this proximity is a drawback because of decreased privacy. The arrival of two additional islands as separate SIMs gave privacy-minded residents an alternative. Yet for financial reasons, the residential land on the center island needed to remain attractive.

For the sake of the residential tenants, primarily, a specific combination of region/estate management tools has been activated. Most areas on the middle island are parceled, including the marketplace as a whole, which gives each residential tenant a great deal of control over his or her land. Flying, building, and terraforming are not available to visitors, which helps keep overly curious passersby out of residential lots. Parceling to this degree also guarantees a prim détente; no merchant can use up the prims allotted to residential tenants, or vice versa.

The depth of residential lots is also crucial to keeping its occupants happy. In general, there's enough space on each lot to build a comfortably sized house while still leaving a 20-meter buffer zone between the village wall and the front door. This is the magic number for privacy; remember, go beyond 20 meters, and you're out of chat range. So most residents on the center island have the option of living closer to the beach and farther away from the banter of marketplace shoppers.

Most homes on Ketora serve strictly one purpose: to be living space for one tenant and his or her "Household." But a few residential lots serve a triple function: the galleon ships. As living space, the galleons offer better privacy for tenants interested in the interior corner lots between two islands. The hulls are tall enough to position windows well out of sight of most people both walking and living nearby. However, the galleons also add significantly to the skyline of all three islands. The masts stand just high enough above the palm trees to draw the eye into the distance, and suggest a wider, more complex vista than what is immediately apparent.

Finally, the galleons act as passive advertising for the second, very large-scale expansion of Ketora. At this writing, **OpenSpace** SIMs have been added to the three main islands, creating a much larger microcontinent. One of these SIMs is the Bay of Ketora, an open-water area where pirate combat is under development. So the galleon ships already in place on Ketora suggested the presence of pirates long before actual ship-to-ship combat became a reality (see Figure 8.20 on the next page).

Public Space Management and Design on Ketora

In non-themed or non-RP areas, public space often serves a handful of simple purposes. It provides a means of ground-level travel, for foot traffic and for vehicles. It delineates different areas of commercial and residential space instead of walls. Some farsighted designers also use public space to hide their prim reserves in plain sight, ensuring that no one in the region will overindulge.

ſLanguage

OpenSpace *n.* Also called *void regions* and *OS SIMs*. A second type of private island offered by Linden Lab, offering four times the usual square meterage as a regular private island, but with only 1,875 prims apiece. OpenSpace SIMs all run on the same server, which may increase lag if they are overcrowded or maxed out in terms of prim usage. In fact, Linden Lab specifically advises against trying to utilize these areas for anything other than boating, greenspace, or "light use." OpenSpace SIMs are also not available as stand-alone SIMs; you can only connect them to a regular island you already own, and you can only get them in groups of four. So for all intents and purposes, OpenSpace SIMs are only available to Second Life residents who already own a private island.

FIGURE 8.20 A galleon ship on Ketora.

FIGURE 8.21 An example of public space on Ketora East: the entry point pavilion on the channel.

By contrast, public space serves a much more complex purpose in themed or role-play SIMs. Public space offers the props and tools for group interactive RP, setting the stage for whatever events or storyline development is going on. "Normal" non-RP behavior usually happens off-stage—on Ketora, behind the village walls on rented residential land. This is in direct contrast to what happens on most public space located elsewhere in Second Life. In SL at large, residents act (mostly) nondescript out in public (see Figure 8.21) and behave otherwise behind closed doors.

From a designer's perspective, this difference in usage comes down to prims. No matter what style you're building, if you are aiming for authenticity of design, you have to decide very carefully and consciously where to "spend" your prims. We've covered all the ways to do this spending in Chapters 7, 8, and earlier here. But in general, everybody else's needs must come first. This is quite frequently the reason why private island owners have no home or homestead of their own. They'd rather use those prims to perfect their overall design or respond to any unanticipated needs of tenants and visitors.

On Ketora, the majority of prims allotted to public space has been spent on landscaping. This was a conscious decision based on the type of climate chosen for the islands, lest Ketora look more like a desert than a beautiful beach. Also, with so much of the land allotted to residential space, where tenants could build in just about any historical style or fashion, Ketora would never have structure in the urban planning sense of the word. This is the reason why most of the public buildings on Ketora are quite plainly constructed. These simple design choices have saved on prims and lessened visual "competition" with the larger, ornate homesteads built by tenants.

Designing for Large-Scale Expansion

The final step in creating the microcontinent of Ketora is the addition of OpenSpace SIMs.

There were multiple, design-related reasons for adding the OpenSpace type of SIM in this particular configuration. In terms of benefit to Ketora specifically, the addition of the OpenSpace areas created the ability for a clear distinction between violent role-play (melee combat) and non-violent role-play (meeting for a drink in the tavern or blue tent). Now, all violent role-play could be hosted in—and restricted to—the new OS areas instead of the plaza. This strategy guaranteed far more tranquility in both the residential and commercial spaces on the original three islands.

The names and positions of all four OS SIMs were also carefully planned (see Figure 8.22). The names suggest the type of combat RP that will take place in each area, giving potential visitors a summary of what to expect with a mere glance at each Search listing. The grouping of each SIM also presents a logical and truly continental shift in climate, from desert (Tahari) to grass (Northern Plains) to woodlands (Northern Forest) and also open sea (Bay of Ketora).

Furthermore, the places where the OS SIMs attach to Ketora East and Ketora West also serve a specific yet dual purpose. The barracks and arena on Ketora East and the harbor/docks on Ketora West work as transition and preparation space (see Figure 8.23).

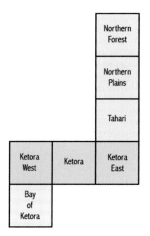

FIGURE 8.22 The plan for all seven SIMs: Ketora at large.

FIGURE 8.23 The barracks and arena on Ketora East.

An entry point has been established in each of these transitional spaces. This allows visitors to get a taste of what lies ahead in each of the OpenSpace SIMs without having to "endanger" themselves. It also gives large traveling or combat parties a place to meet up and prepare for venturing forth. Also, the barracks/arena and harbor/docks are surrounded by rentable residential space. It is easy to see if any of this space is available, if visiting turns into an opportunity for renting.

The final, and possibly most important, function of the OpenSpace SIMs is to provide linkage points for other Gorean SIMs to attach to Ketora. At this writing, two non-Ketoran Gorean regions are being created and will join to the microcontinent. This evolution makes it possible to recreate a more authentic feeling of travel across Gor, for example, walking, riding horses, riding in carts, and such, but not teleporting. It also makes Ketora a truly cooperative role-playing experience, unique among not only the Gorean RP population within Second Life but also in SL as a whole.

The Near Future of Second Life

As Second Life continues to grow, it will continue to embrace and be embraced by other forms of media and by more people. So this type of collective approach to a single, though general, goal is quite likely in the future. SL began as a mass communal experience and will continue to head in that direction, as long as the technology, the creativity, and the will of its residents remains wide open to possibilities.

> ### ADDITIONAL CREDITS
>
> You can find all the brand, style, color, and designer information on items shown in the figures in the online appendix you get when registering your book at at www.peachpit.com/secondlife. See page v for details.

INDEX

makeup tips, 36
male shapes, 30–32, 52
Map
    illustrated, 13
    showing destinations on, 12
    surveying local land prices with, 144–145
    tracking friends on, 106–107
measuring
    development space, 178–179, 190, 191
    Second Life base measurements, 26
    traffic, 115
meeting spaces, 183
menus
    drop-down, 8, 9
    Pie, 10
microcontinents. *See also* Ketora
    defined, 15
mixed land zoning, 90
modify/no modify permissions, 48
money. *See* Linden dollars
Mouselook, 139–140
multi-item vendors, 183
My Notes tab page (Profile dialog box), 78–79

N

nail polish, 36
names
    avatar, 24
    defined, 68
    region and estate, 175
naughty bits, 33, 69
night, 167, 168
non-human avatars, 39–41
Norman, John, 121, 189

O

objects. *See also* attachments
    AOs, 101
    constructing with Build tools, 138–139
    defined, 131
    duplicating, 140
    editing linked parts, 166
    emptying from Trash, 132
    occlusion of, 38
    permissions to edit and delete, 107
    resizing, 133, 135
    saving built, 21
    selecting Build, 133
occlusion, 38
online shopping sites, 58–59
OOC (out of character), 119, 164
OpenSpace SIMs, 199, 201–202

Options tab page (About Land dialog box), 77
orientation tools, 138
out of character (OOC), 119, 164

P

parcels, 15, 180
partnerships, 110–111. *See also* relationships
part-time work, 114, 115
Path Cut tool, 148
People tab page (Search dialog box), 91–92
performance
    effect of megaprims and temp-rezzers on, 134
    lag and popular places, 86–88
    number of residents and server, 70
    private islands and, 173
    vendor types and, 183
permissions
    clothing, 48, 53
    giving friend, 106, 107–108
personas, 67–93
    About: Text box summarizing, 72
    creating your Profile, 68–79
    information found on 2nd Life tab, 69, 71–72
    searching for other residents, 79–81
    viewing Profiles, 68, 69
photos, size of Profile, 71, 74
Pick: Color dialog box, 167
Pick: Texture dialog box, 64, 137
Picks tab page (Profile dialog box), 73–75
Pie menu
    about, 10
    Detach All option, 39
    Profile option on, 68
Places tab page (Search dialog box), 91–92
planning
    approximating layout during, 180–181
    brainstorming designs, 179–180, 190–193
    commercial spaces, 181–183
    expansion using OS SIMs, 201–202
    Ketora's development guidelines, 189–190
    landscaping, 151–152
    measuring development space, 178–179, 190, 191
    private island development, 176–177
plants, 155–158
Play in World/Play Locally options (Animation dialog box), 101
polling, 115
Popular Places tab page (Search dialog box), 86–88
poseballs
    childbearing, 111
    defined, 130
    naughty, 108, 130